Making Faith-Sense

Theological Reflection in Everyday Life

Robert L. Kinast

A Liturgical Press Book

THE LITURGICAL PRESS
Collegeville, Minnesota

Cover design by Greg Becker

9   10   11   12   13

Library of Congress Cataloging-in-Publication Data

Kinast, Robert L.
    Making faith-sense : theological reflection in everyday life /
Robert L. Kinast.
        p. cm.
    ISBN 0-8146-2513-4 (alk. paper)
    1. Spirituality—Catholic Church.   I. Title.
BX2350.65.K57   1999
248.4—dc21
                                                      98-46238
                                                          CIP

To my mother and father
whose faith always made sense of their life

To my brother, Don,
whose sense of life comes from his faith

To Judith,
who knows how life makes sense of faith

Contents

Introduction

Making faith-sense is a new term for an ancient practice. It is what the early Christians called mystical or wisdom theology—an understanding of life in the light of God's participation in it. They did not think of this as an intellectual skill or task reserved only for specially trained scholars. Making faith-sense was the way of life for a disciple of Jesus. It coincided with his call, recorded in the gospels, to recognize the signs of God's presence in everyday events and to shape one's life accordingly. As people did this, they guided their lives into the reign of God, or to put it more biblically, God reigned in their lives.

The purpose of this book is to continue that tradition. It describes a step-by-step process to help you figure out where God is and what God is up to in your life, and to respond appropriately. This has always been a challenging task, but it is even more so today because of two major developments that go back to the Age of the Enlightenment (seventeenth and eighteenth centuries). You may already be familiar with this background or you may feel you do not need it at this point. If so, please proceed to chapter one. If you want to come back to this material later, it will be here for you to read.

The Enlightenment laid the groundwork for much of modern culture in the West, including democratic forms of government and recognition of individual human rights. However, it is also severely criticized for fostering an extreme individualism which threatens to fragment society and allow each person to be the sole arbiter of what is right and wrong, true and false, beautiful and ugly—in short, to decide what makes sense and what does not.

In the religious sphere this extreme individualism appears as the privatizing of religion. In this view, instead of the public revelation of God, proclaimed and handed on by the institutional Church, people have inner, private experiences of God and on this basis live their lives of faith. The Church is little more than an association of individuals, each of whom decides for himself or herself what to believe and how to act. The classic indication of privatized religion is that no believer can speak for another; the contemporary expression of it is the rise of New Age spirituality.

Turn to the Subject

Although the Enlightenment did foster a strong sense of individualism, it did so as part of a twofold emphasis which is both positive and necessary. The first emphasis has been called a "turn to the subject." It represents the Enlightenment's rebellion against what it perceived as excessive control of individuals by the prevailing institutions of the time—the monarchy, the Church, and the wealthy. Instead of conforming to the authority and decisions of these institutions and their representatives (which became increasingly self-serving), the Enlightenment urged every person to think and act for themselves. In effect, it restored the value and validity of personal experience over against the formal, traditional, or generic determinations of how everyone should live.

The Enlightenment's turn to the subject led to a recognition of both the rights and the responsibilities of each person as a human being. In subsequent history the former have been championed much more strenuously than the latter but both are included in the turn to the subject. A person not only has inalienable rights that are to be protected by law and social practice, but each person also has a responsibility to achieve the maximum fulfillment possible, given one's experience of life and desire for improvement. The Enlightenment ideal was that the self-determined success of each individual would yield the greatest benefit for the common good.

Although this ideal may seem naive in light of human sinfulness (and post-Enlightenment history), the turn to the subject was intended to give each person the authority and freedom they deserved to live a meaningful life, i.e., a life that made sense in relation to their circumstances and ideals. In this respect at least, the Enlightenment is not far removed from the thrust of Jesus' preaching and ministry.

As portrayed in the gospels, Jesus appealed directly to the people he encountered, affirming their value as children of God and alerting them to the ways that God's reign was inviting them to live in freedom and dignity. In effect he tried to liberate them from the controlling influences that kept them from experiencing the fullness of God's life available to them right in their midst. Sometimes these controlling influences were cast as demons (Matt 8:28-34), sometimes as social stereotypes (John 9:1-3), sometimes as misleading interpretations of the Law (Luke 6:6-11), sometimes as erroneous religious practices (Matthew 23). When pressed for evidence about the validity of his ministry, Jesus turned to the subjects he had affected and let their experience speak for itself: the blind see, the lame walk, lepers are cleansed, the deaf hear, the dead are raised to life, and the poor hear good news (Luke 7:18-23).

Critical Thinking

The second emphasis of the Enlightenment was critical thinking. As part of the rebellion against traditional authority (especially the dogmas of the churches and the religious wars they fostered) and consistent with the turn to the subject, the Enlightenment extolled the power of human reason and urged people to think for themselves. Often this meant to think like the leaders of the Enlightenment, but the ideal of liberated reason launched a new era in critical thinking which has not abated.

Critical thinking does not mean simply negative criticism of established teachings and convictions; in fact, it may not include negative criticism at all. Critical thinking means an honest search for the truth by comparing different positions, questioning their bases and assumptions, analyzing their sources, testing their implications, and forming judgments about their validity and relevance. This is understood to be an ongoing process in which no one has a final or complete grasp of the truth.

This type of critical thinking follows the turn to the subject. When people take their own experience seriously and find

Making Faith-Sense

discrepancies between it and official (or conventional, established) thinking and practice, they raise questions, examine motives and assumptions, and try to make sense of the differences they perceive. In one sense this was the strategy behind many of Jesus' parables.

Jesus constructed situations that were familiar to his hearers (and with slight variations, familiar in today's world as well): a traveler is robbed, a son goes astray, a sheep is lost, a dinner invitation arrives, workers are paid at the end of the day, a widow persists in getting a just legal settlement, a man falls into serious debt, tenants take advantage of the owner's absence. Then he drew his listeners inside the story so they would have to make a decision for themselves, comparing their personal experience with official interpretations of the Law: help the robbery victim or remain ritually pure? welcome back the son or make him pay the consequences? stay with the ninety-nine or seek the one? take care of personal needs first or honor another's invitation? conduct business by strict policy or generosity? do what is right or act expediently? be compassionate or take advantage of another's misfortune? act with integrity or exploit a situation for personal gain?

In Jesus' parables, answers were never self-evident; they demanded honest reflection and personal decision. Similarly, critical thinking does not mean looking for reasons to justify a course of action you have already decided to take; it means examining a situation carefully in order to determine the course of action you should take.

Making faith-sense is located within this tradition of personal, critical reflection on experience. It is not simply declaring what you think "because that's my experience," as if nothing else matters. It is not simply doing what you want "because that's my decision," as if no one else is involved or affected. Making faith-sense does rely on personal experience and it does require personal decisions, but both are imbedded in a tradition and interact with the people, beliefs, rituals, and systems we have inherited. How you may accomplish this is the purpose of the following chapters.

☙ CHAPTER ONE ❧

What Is Faith-Sense?

Mike had a good-paying job in a well-established company but he handed in his resignation and moved his family to Wyoming to take over a cattle ranch. "It just doesn't make sense," his co-workers commented. "He had everything going for him here. Why would he make such a drastic change?"

Cheryl had been an effective leader in school and church organizations while her children were growing up, so she decided to run for the local school board. "It makes sense that she would take her experience and commitment to the next level," friends agreed when they heard the news.

Bill and Beverly turned seventy, sold their house, bought a mobile home, and began criss-crossing the country visiting their married children and grandchildren. Their eldest son thought it made great sense for his parents to travel while they could and do what they enjoyed most—being with family. His younger sisters thought it made no sense at all for seventy-year-olds to be on the go like this, especially if they should face medical or financial problems.

These examples, and countless others like them, illustrate a familiar fact: what you do is supposed to make sense. Your decisions and your actions are expected to be consistent with the values, principles, goals, and beliefs people hold in common. And most people are quite ready to judge whether you have acted sensibly or not. Of course, what makes sense to one person or group might not make sense to another.

It may not make sense to parents that their son or daughter wants to quit college and live in a community of artists but it makes perfect sense to the aspiring painter, poet, or musician. It may not make sense to people in a pleasure-seeking society that there are communities of individuals who abstain from food, alcohol, sex, and material comfort, but it makes sense to them in their quest for a spiritual life. There is a lot of room for individuality, variety, and difference of opinion within the range of typical sources people use to make sense of their lives.

Sources for Making Sense of Life

The first and most familiar source for making sense of life is *common sense*. Common sense is a set of convictions that seem self-evident to most people. Dress warmly in cold weather; do not write checks for more money than you have in your bank account; be sure you have enough time to prepare a meal if you are inviting friends over for dinner. These truths are so obvious that they are rarely stated explicitly, until you violate them. Then you will hear comments like: "Common sense would tell you to wear a coat in freezing temperatures" or "Where was your common sense when you wrote those checks?"

In addition to common sense, and usually reinforcing it, is *family sense*. These are the customs, traditions, standards (and sometimes secrets) that define and distinguish individual families. Children born into the family or spouses who marry into it are expected to learn the family's way of making sense. This may be conveyed in pithy statements such as "Kennedy boys don't quit," "our family does not accept charity," "Hatfields don't mingle with McCoys." It may also be communicated in unspoken expectations and rules such as: everyone celebrates the holidays at the family home; no one talks about Uncle Walt who lived by himself on a sheep farm and committed suicide. The reasons behind these family traditions are not always clearly expressed or even understood, but members of the family are expected to conform to them in making sense of their lives.

Your *ethnic and cultural background* provides a third source for making sense. An Irish wake, a Polish or Italian wedding, a Jewish bar mitzvah, a German Christmas or African-American kwanza, a Chinese new year, a Mexican fiesta all celebrate common life events, but they do so in distinctive ways that might not make sense to someone from another culture. Similarly, education helps you make sense of life as you gain knowledge and acquire a school spirit; athletics does the same through teamwork, fair play, and competition; voluntary associations help through specific causes, self-giving, and socializing.

For most people, the world of *work* is a fourth influential source for making sense. Earning a living, providing products or services for others, adapting to changes in the work- and marketplace are all part of the process of making sense of life. Many businesses try to create a company culture and train workers in their way of doing things. Profit and loss statements, the value of stockholder shares, rating systems, and business awards all signal how a company makes sense of its place in the economy. Companies use slogans and logos to convince customers they can help make sense of their lives. A pest company declares, "Life is too short to be bugged." A newspaper promises "all the information you need." A hospital proclaims, "Your health is our care."

Making Faith-Sense

Of course, churches and religious organizations have their own view of what makes sense. This is where making *faith*-sense comes into play. Making faith-sense means fitting one's life into the pattern of faith values, beliefs, and ideals that have been handed on from previous generations. However, "fitting in" does not mean slavish conformity to the past or rationalizing your actions artificially. It means creating a personal, practical way of living, consistent with a faith view of life. This is not always easy.

For example, Jerry and Pat are wrestling with whether to send their children to public schools in order to support local integration efforts or to make the personal and financial sacrifices required to send the children to private schools where they may perhaps gain a better education. Wanda, a single mother, must decide whether to accept a promotion that would offer financial security and advance her professional career but would require time away from home and her two teenage children. Dave, a conscientious voter, wants to support his state legislator because she works hard for the unemployed, the elderly, and young people, but she also supports abortion rights which Dave opposes.

In an imperfect world it is not always clear which decision makes the best sense, even for people of faith.

Adding to this challenge is the fact that the values, beliefs, and ideals that people use to make faith-sense of their lives are not timeless, static concepts. They are living realities, embodied in the people, rituals, teachings, and structures which address the changing circumstances of every age. It took Christians nearly a thousand years to recognize and declare the sacramentality of marriage even though its sacredness as a sign of Christ's union with the Church had been proclaimed by St. Paul from the outset (Eph 5:21-33). The association of labor with punishment for original sin dominated Church thinking until the misery and unjust working conditions of the modern industrial age called for a defense of worker's rights and the articulation of a spirituality of work.

Just as people make sense of their lives with the help of common sense and the other sources mentioned above, so people of faith draw upon a kind of *spiritual common sense* as well as other sources of faith. Spiritual common sense is the sense of the faith given by the Holy Spirit to the people of God as a whole. With this sense of the faith Christians know that they are not just individuals with a private relationship to God but members of a community and tradition of belief. They know they are to be fair and charitable in their dealings with others, even when they disagree or face persecution. They know they should be generous in helping the poor and those in need, faithful to the commitments they make, and consistent in practicing the principles of justice in work and society.

People of faith usually belong to a specific *denomination* which also influences their faith-sense. This is somewhat akin to the family traditions in which people are raised. Denominational traditions give a particular shape to the broad Christian faith through distinctive emphases and practices. For example, people raised in the Catholic traditions (Roman, Orthodox, Anglican) usually emphasize ritual liturgy, sacraments, and hierarchical structure, whereas people raised in the Protestant reform traditions (Lutheran, Presbyterian, Methodist, Baptist) usually have a keen sense of personal prayer, biblical preaching, and individual witness. Of course, denominational differences occurred in the first place because of conflicting attempts to make sense of Christianity when disputes arose among Christians. Denominations are a historical testimony to the difficulty and dynamics of making faith-sense.

These denominational differences are sometimes sharpened by *cultural additions* which can often co-exist cross-culturally. A typical Catholic parish may include devotions to the Infant Jesus of Prague (Czech Republic), the Miraculous Medal and first Fridays (France), the first Saturdays (Portugal), the Advent wreath (Germany), Our Lady of Guadalupe (Mexico), and the Stations of the Cross (the Holy Land by way of medieval Europe). Southern Baptist preaching is likely to have a regional style and idiom that differs noticeably from Northern Baptist preaching. Special prestige may be attached to belonging to the Cathedral or the "first" Baptist, Presbyterian, Methodist church in a town. All of these ethnic and cultural variations influence the way church members make faith-sense of their experience.

The place of religion and specifically of Christianity in *society* also affects the way people make faith-sense. In the U.S. the best known example of this is the constitutional prohibition of a state-established religion, popularly rendered as the separation of Church and state. This political arrangement is often interpreted to mean that religion is a private matter and has no public role—which, of course, is one way of making faith-sense. In fact, the original intention was to allow all religious groups to exert a public influence without government preference being given to one favored group—which is another way of making faith-sense.

The depiction of religion in the entertainment media is a further cultural influence on making faith-sense. The portrayal of evangelicals, Catholics, and Jews may or may not accurately reflect their way of making faith-sense but it does create an impression which in turn affects the way believing people make faith-sense of their lives—defensively, self-consciously, confidently, counter-culturally.

Meaning and Facts

Making faith-sense, like making sense of any kind, tries to honor the twin claims of *meaning* and *facts*. This is the final piece in a definition of making faith-sense. Meaning is roughly equivalent to or located on the subjective side of a situation. It refers to how you feel about the birth of your child, a promotion (or firing) at work, the election of a new president. Facts are on the objective side. They refer to the demographics and experience of families today, the rate of employment and the prospects for new jobs, the record of public officials and the final votes for each candidate.

Although meaning and facts constantly influence each other, they are not the same thing. A meaningful relationship may not be what it seems if the other person turns out to be abusive or an alcoholic. A job that appears ideal may actually exploit you, your co-workers, your customers, or poor people. A cultural development that looks promising may prove to be deceptive, as with the claims for certain medicines and diet programs, the promise of a political movement, the lure of unregulated investment opportunities.

On the other hand, a relationship may be exactly as it appears (that is, true to the facts) but not very meaningful because the other person is boring, opinionated, or manipulative. A job may really be lucrative and prestigious but stifling, time consuming, and frustrating. A new movie or TV show might be exactly as advertised but superficial and offensive to your values.

Connecting meaning with facts is a challenge in the Church, too. Doctrines and practices may be factually true but irrelevant to your life. The finer points of a theology of grace, the intellectual struggle to understand the Trinity, or the classic debates about faith and works may not help you make much faith-sense of your responsibilities as a parent, a worker, or a citizen. On the other hand, your desire for a meaningful spiritual experience (such as sharing communion with other denominations) may not be true to the facts (the churches are still divided). These challenges are compounded by the fact that people's needs and desires keep changing throughout their lifetime, from generation to generation, and from culture to culture. The Baltimore Catechism that served American Catholics well from its approval in the late nineteenth century (1885) had to be updated after Vatican II by the Catechism of the Catholic Church (1992). Liturgical rites and lectionaries developed by separate denominations need to be replaced by common rites and assigned readings in an ecumenical age. Making faith-sense tries to wed meaning and facts. You can start with either one, but it is important to include the claims of both.

It is clear from this brief overview that making faith-sense is not a simple, automatic activity. It requires thought, effort, and a desire to derive the maximum benefit from your experience as a believing person. To do this, it is important to have a method or series of steps you can follow to facilitate your attempts at making faith-sense. That is the purpose of the following chapters.

☙ CHAPTER TWO ❧

How to Make Faith-Sense: Getting Started

To make faith-sense of everyday experience, you should start with everyday experience. That sounds obvious (which it is) and fairly easy (which it is not). Experience does not come in neatly defined segments, like TV shows or work hours. It flows, one event merging into and overlapping another.

Your alarm goes off and before you know it, you've awakened the children for school, taken a shower, eaten breakfast, glanced at the morning paper, and gotten dressed. You may car pool to school or work, run some errands, and make a few phone calls before things get really hectic. During all of this you may be wondering what to cook for dinner, how to avoid an obnoxious co-worker who always wants to go to lunch, and where you are going to get a baby sitter for Friday night.

And so it goes throughout the day. Some things are planned and carried out; others are interrupted or postponed; still others happen unexpectedly and spontaneously. There may be surprises, disappointments, routines, stress, and overload. You may be called upon to exercise your role as a parent, spouse, worker, friend, neighbor, citizen, volunteer, and believer. You may make conversation, plans, decisions, purchases, and love. You may give advice, offer prayers, pay bills, and do your job.

Of course, there are people whose days seem empty, monotonous, and lonely. Elderly people who live alone, persons with a chronic illness or disability, prison inmates, poor people and the unemployed may not have much to do or experience from one day to the next. No matter, whatever goes on in your life is part of the continuous stream of everyday experience which beckons you to make sense of it.

The instinctive way most people handle the steady flow of events that make up their experience is to block them off, name them, and deal with them as if they were separate, clearly defined things—this morning's business meeting, this afternoon's appointment with the doctor, this evening's movie. This is a monumental achievement of practicality. It enables you to focus on certain things (presumably the important ones) and disregard or subordinate the rest, even though all of it belongs together and makes up your total experience. This is a key step in making any sense of experience, and it is just as important in making faith-sense. You must keep in mind, however, that some of the events that precede a particular experience and some which follow it may be very important for understanding and making sense of that experience.

For example, your son may appear to be pouting and sullen after you tell him to clean his room. You may think he is resisting your parental authority but he is actually reacting to a disappointment at school that day. Your boss may be unusually upbeat and complimentary at the weekly sales meeting. You think it is because you are all doing a good job but it is really because he just learned that the growth on his neck is not malignant.

You do not need to become an amateur psychologist or investigative reporter, looking for hidden motives in everything that happens, but you do have to be aware that there is more to each event than first appears. That is why reflection is required to make satisfactory sense of everyday experience.

Selecting an Experience

Bearing this in mind, where do you begin among all the experiences which make up your life? Three suggestions can guide your choice.

1. Start with *a recent experience,* something that happened within the last few days. For example, in the mail the other day

a handmade card arrived announcing the birth of a baby boy to Michelle and her husband. I have known Michelle most of her life and her parents are among my closest friends, although we live in different cities and rarely see each other. I was about to send a congratulations card to Michelle when I realized I had thrown away the envelope with her new address. I called her parents to get it. To my surprise they were both at home and we had a wonderful half-hour conversation, celebrating the birth of their latest grandchild, talking about their experience of recent retirement, catching up on other events, and tentatively planning to get together when they vacation nearby.

What is the advantage in selecting a recent experience like this? Recent experiences are still fresh in the memory and fairly easy to recall. I can remember the things my friends and I talked about, the people we mentioned, the memories we shared, the changes that have occurred since last we talked (they now have e-mail and we exchanged electronic addresses). Having this kind of fairly complete grasp of an experience is an important part of making faith-sense, as will be explained below.

Recent experiences also have an impact as you continue to feel their effects, and this too is important in making faith-sense. As a result of our phone conversation, I feel reconnected with my friends and reaffirmed in our relationship. I have recalled times we shared together in the past, especially during the years when Michelle was growing up. The phone conversation lasted thirty minutes; its effects have continued for more than a week.

Finally, recent experiences remain "alive" to some degree; their meaning is still taking shape and can be enriched by the reflection that goes into making faith-sense. I wrote a longer personal note to Michelle than I probably would have otherwise, reminiscing about her childhood and thanking her for including me in the joy of her motherhood. To me, this felt like a variation on the biblical blessing of seeing your children's children to the third and fourth generation.

I am also looking forward to seeing my friends again soon and we have already exchanged e-mail messages, verifying in this instance at least that computer technology can enhance human relationships. In an obvious sense I simply lost the envelope with the return address I needed. In a faith-sense, what I lost was restored as a renewal of friendship and shared life—not the whole meaning of redemption, to be sure, but a small example of it in my recent experience.

Recent experiences are a helpful way to begin, but making faith-sense is not confined to recent events. As you develop a facility for reflecting on recent experiences, you can go back to events that are more removed in time and make sense of them from a faith perspective. This is especially important for decisive moments which continue to influence your life, or traumatic events which you have never quite dealt with.

For example, Chuck is in his early forties, a devout Christian, and the father of five children. He was hired as operations director by a company whose purpose is to train and employ underskilled workers. This social mission appealed very much to Chuck and was a major motivation in his acceptance of the job. However, after three years the company decided he was not meeting their expectations and released him.

Chuck and his wife, Eileen, were devastated. They felt this was exactly what the Lord wanted them to do and they could not understand what his dismissal meant. However, they did not have time to reflect on this event (not even to draw biblical parallels with the stories of Abraham and Sarah, Jacob and Rachel, Mary and Joseph, who were all unexpectedly uprooted and forced to move on). Chuck had to find a new job to support his family. When he did, it was in a different city. This meant selling one house, buying another, and relocating while keeping the family intact and paying the bills. Eventually, Chuck and Eileen will have time to reflect on all this and try to make faith-sense of it. If they have developed a facility for making faith-sense of recent experiences, they will be in a better position to grapple with this major event in their lives.

At the same time, your skill in reflecting on past events (whether recent or remote) can help you make faith-sense of events as they are happening. This enriches the experience as it is occurring and makes it even more meaningful when you reflect on it later. One example of this is the experience of attending a play or a movie with friends and discussing it afterwards. During the performance you undoubtedly react to the story, the characters, the action in terms of your values and beliefs. After the performance, as you discuss it with your friends, you may recognize things you missed during the show or see them more clearly than you did at the time. Moving back and forth like this between current and past events helps to make faith-sense of everything that happens in your life.

2. *Pay attention to your feelings.* Events that arouse your emotions engage you, draw something out of you, connect with something important in you. They suggest that some insight into your faith is waiting to be made and with it perhaps a closer relationship with your God. Among all your recent experiences, which ones grabbed you emotionally? When did you feel the strongest emotions (joy, anger, compassion, fear, satisfaction)?

For example, Paula and her husband recently took his mother in to live with them and their three children. It has been a strain for everyone, especially Paula. This is not how she envisioned her marriage and family life unfolding. One day she went grocery shopping just to get out of the house and relieve her stress. The gentleman who bagged her groceries was walking her to the car and she asked him if he liked working at the store. He said it was all right but he had really hoped to be a vendor at the new ball park downtown. He explained that he had passed all the admission tests but when he went on the day of hiring, he was told they did not need him. "They said they made a random selection of qualified applicants, but I know they just didn't want anybody my age working there."

Paula could not get the man's comment out of her mind. He seemed so sad and rejected. She felt angry that he had been treated this way (assuming his version of what happened was correct), grateful that she and her husband could provide a happy home for her mother-in-law, and a little apprehensive about her own old age even though it was decades away.

Feelings like these are the best indicator of the value, importance, and meaning of things that happen in your life. Events that do not evoke an emotional reaction probably are not very meaningful—at least, not to you. Paula had no particular feelings about shopping for groceries; it was part of her weekly routine and on this occasion it got her out of the house for a while. However, one of the other shoppers that day was a young man in a wheel chair who has chronic multiple sclerosis. Despite this, he was shopping for himself. To him, the tedious and time-consuming act of buying his own groceries was extremely meaningful. Feelings also provide a preliminary boundary to your experience. They block off the people, circumstances, and exchanges that distinguish one experience from another. Additional facts which help to explain why you felt as you did can be added later, but initially your emotional reaction highlights the slice of experience you want to reflect on. If Paula were to make faith-sense of her experience, she would probably not mention shopping except as the occasion for her exchange with the man who bagged her groceries. Her encounter with him is the real experience she wants to make faith-sense of, as she draws out its implications for the way society treats the elderly and how she wants to treat her mother-in-law.

3. *Pay attention to your thoughts and conversation.* If you find yourself thinking and talking a lot about a certain event, you probably sense that it contains meaning that you want to grasp more clearly. When a contemporary of mine died recently after a three-year struggle with cancer, I found myself talking about him with people who had never met him, exchanging stories and anecdotes with mutual friends, recalling experiences we had shared together, using phrases that were typical of him, and citing incidents from his life as examples in lectures and writing (including my reference to him now). When this happens, as it frequently does after someone's death, it is a good indication that the experience is beckoning you to explore its meaning and make faith-sense of it.

Paying attention to your thoughts and conversation is actually another way of paying attention to your feelings, but it may be more effective for you if you are not accustomed to attending to your feelings as a clue to the spiritual and theological meaning of your life. If you were raised with the notion that religion is all doctrine and obligation, it may even seem strange to initiate the search for faith-sense by concentrating on your feelings. If this is the case, then observing your thoughts and conversation topics may be a more friendly way of achieving the goal of selecting a

recent event you want to reflect on because it engages you and invites you to make faith-sense of it.
To concretize these suggestions, consider the following example.

Henrietta was correcting her last exam paper when her husband, Rich, called down from their bedroom, "I think you'll want to watch the eleven o'clock news tonight." Henrietta was puzzled. She never watched TV news, preferring to get her information from the morning paper— when she had time to read it. Rich explained. "The school board voted tonight to rescind the busing plan."

Henrietta has been an elementary grade teacher in the public school system for fifteen years. She is committed to working with children from economically poor areas of the city, convinced that a quality education is their only hope for advancement. For the last five years she has taught at a magnet school to which black and Hispanic children are bused.

The news report described how the school board had voted five to one to terminate the busing plan, and the magnet school system that went with it. In the judgment of the school board the original plan, now twenty-five years in place, had achieved its purpose of racial balance and educational parity. Not only was the magnet school no longer needed, it was actually counterproductive because it perpetuated the impression of racial animosity and inequality.

"They can't possibly believe that," Henrietta said in anger and disbelief as she listened to the report. She felt herself being pulled by her emotions in several directions at once: outrage at the reasoning of the board, sympathy with the children affected and their parents, anxiety about her own future in the school system, frustration at not being able to do anything, impatience with the political issues influencing the board's decision, discouragement at the persistent inequalities she experiences first-hand, and futility at the thought that her efforts for the last fifteen years may have been wasted.

Over the next few days, all Henrietta could think about was the school board's vote. When friends or neighbors casually asked her how things were going, she would launch into a full discussion of the board's action and her view of it. She read every article about it in the newspaper, including letters to the editor which she ordinarily never read. She even listened to radio call-in shows to find out what people were saying.

A week after the decision, Henrietta and Rich attended the meeting of their parish prayer group. As part of the format, each person mentioned one request for prayers for a particular intention. Henrietta had no difficulty selecting the experience she wanted to bring to the group. When she did, they were not only empathetic and supportive, but they helped her begin to make faith-sense of the experience. Some suggested biblical parallels such as Jesus' struggle with the biases of his time and St. Paul's trials in spreading the gospel. Others recalled that work for justice is one of the most frustrating ways to practice your faith, and one person mentioned that this is why the cross is the preeminent symbol of Christian discipleship.

These suggestions were prompted by the fact that Henrietta had shared a recent experience which engaged her emotionally and dominated her thoughts and conversation. That is the best kind of experience for making faith-sense.

EXERCISE

When you want to make faith-sense of your experience, begin by recalling the events of the past several days. Select one of them, taking the following points into account.

1. Is the experience recent? (The school board's vote was within the last week.)
2. Did the experience elicit your emotions? (Henrietta felt anger, disbelief, outrage, sympathy, anxiety, frustration, impatience, discouragement, and futility.)
3. Have you thought about the incident very often or talked about it with others since it occurred? (Henrietta could deal with little else; she talked to anyone who would listen and listened to anyone who expressed a viewpoint; and she brought her experience to the prayer group for their reactions and support.)

If your experience matches these criteria, it is a good place to begin making faith-sense.

Helpful Resources

Making faith-sense is more than putting a few ideas together or simply reacting to things that happen. It is thoughtful, deliberate consideration of your experience. For Chuck and Eileen to make faith-sense of his dismissal from a company they thought the Lord wanted him to work for, they will need to do more than affirm that God's ways are mysterious or that everything works out for the best. They will need to probe their experience of disappointment when they thought they were doing the Lord's will and reassess how they determine what God is asking of them. To achieve this kind of reflection, two resources are especially helpful: time and partners.

1. Making faith-sense requires *time*. How much time cannot be predetermined. You can make faith-sense of some experiences with very little reflection. An in-depth analysis is not required to grasp the spiritual meaning of a baby's birth to parents whose family are your lifelong friends eager to share their happiness with you. Other experiences are more complex and their faith meaning is somewhat hidden. Paula's encounter with the man who bagged her groceries has many implications for Paula, her husband and children, the man himself, Paula's mother-in-law, and society as a whole. It will take longer than her drive home or a few minutes' conversation with her husband while unpacking the groceries for Paula to make adequate faith-sense of that event.

To make faith-sense effectively, it helps to set aside time (even fifteen minutes will do) and use it in a methodical way (to be explained below). Of course, it also helps to set aside time when you are alert and reasonably free of distractions, but you cannot always control that. If you are like most thoughtful believers, you undoubtedly already reflect on the faith meaning of events in your life, but you probably do so sporadically, when you have a few moments before falling asleep, while taking a shower, driving to work, listening to the Sunday homily. The purpose of this chapter, and the reason for presenting it gradually, step-by-step, is to help you make maximum use of the time you do have.

2. The second resource for making faith-sense is a *partner,* or partners. Christianity is not a private religion and making faith-sense is not supposed to be a solitary exercise. It works best when it is a shared reflection, although you should not feel obliged to make faith-sense with other people, especially if you find it difficult to share personal experiences or if you do not have other people readily available to talk with. Private reflection is always a valuable and necessary ingredient in living a meaningful faith life. Nonetheless, a special dynamic occurs when you tell another person your experience. You often hear it and feel it differently when you communicate it out loud.

A humorous example of this are advertisements that portray a young man rehearsing how to express his feelings to his girl friend or fiancée. All the practice in the world is no preparation for the face-to-face moment (when, of course, the right soft drink, deodorant, or greeting card makes everything turn out perfectly). Fantasy aside, the point is that the actual communication of your experience to another person can reveal aspects of the experience that you would not have recognized by yourself.

For example, when Emily was promoted to district manager, she could hardly wait to tell her husband, Sam, and their friends. As she talked about her new status and responsibilities, she also heard herself say that she would now be able to implement the idea of co-workers treating one another as internal customers. This was something she always felt was lacking in the company's training program and in the actual conduct of employees toward one another. But until she verbalized it, she had not realized that this was a big part of what the promotion meant to her.

There are other reasons why partners are helpful in making faith-sense. If you have selected a recent meaningful experience (one which aroused your emotions and you have thought or talked about a lot), it may well offer more meaning than you can discover by yourself. Partners who know you, share your faith perspective, and are willing to explore your experience with you can help you uncover these additional meanings, which may prove more beneficial to you than the insights you gain by yourself.

When Emily mentioned the idea of internal customers to one of her friends, her friend did not know what Emily was talking about. Emily explained that workers in her company are trained to be courteous, responsive, and helpful to paying customers but are allowed to be curt, insensitive, and gossipy toward one another. Emily wants to train the people in her district to treat one another as if they were customers, because they are. They are internal customers. Her friend said that Emily's description reminded her of the old saying, "Charity begins at home, and nobody does that better than you do."

Until that moment, Emily had not thought of her business approach in terms of charity or the values of her faith. The more she reflected on it though, the more she realized that she did try to treat everyone with respect and affirm them as persons. Her promotion at work suddenly took on a whole new meaning as her friend helped her make faith-sense of it.

Partners can also keep you honest if you start to shy away from uncomfortable implications in your experience or interpret it in a self-serving way. People do not have to be trained counselors to do this. Just by sharing their own reactions to your interpretation and offering their insights into your experience, they provide a sounding board for your reflection.

When Emily told her younger brother, a social worker, about her promotion and how she planned to use her new position, he congratulated her sincerely, then added, "I bet the extra money and status don't hurt either." It was not a sarcastic or cutting remark, but it made Emily face the fact that she felt a lot of ego gratification in her promotion. She realized there was nothing wrong with feeling good about herself and her accomplishments, but she also realized she did not want to let it go to her head or change her self image, much less her values. Without her little brother's comment, Emily might have overlooked the pitfalls of climbing the corporate ladder.

Partners also keep you going when you do not want to make the effort; they often provide a stimulus when you are stuck or unable to find much meaning in your experience. Three months into her new position Emily was feeling a lot of frustration. Her efforts to encourage better relationships among employees were not meeting with much success and many of the male workers resented having a woman as their supervisor. She felt only half-hearted support from her vice president at the corporate office who reminded her somewhat condescendingly that the purpose of their company was to make a profit, not to make employees feel good.

When Emily shared this experience with the friend who had told her that charity begins at home, her friend drew a parallel with Emily's two children. "They're darling kids," she said, "but I know they don't do what you tell them or meet your expectations all the time, and yet I don't hear you talking about firing them." Emily had to laugh at the notion of firing her family, but it helped her realize that getting people to change their behavior is hard work. Harder, it seems, when they are asked to change for the better. With the encouragement of her friend and drawing on her family experience, Emily renewed her efforts to pursue the goal she knew was right, in both a business and a faith sense.

Most of all, partners remind you that you and your experience are part of a community of believers, and the task of making faith-sense has a long history with numerous participants. Partners can put you in touch with people and resources, past and present, who have been helpful to them and may be helpful to you. One Sunday during the time when Emily was feeling so frustrated, she and her family were returning from church, discussing the Scripture lessons and homily they had just heard. The gospel reading was from Mark 4:30-34, the parable of the mustard seed which grew to become a great tree giving shade to the birds.

"I've always liked that parable," said Sam, a fifteen-year government employee. "There are so many times when I wonder whether my input has any effect on a report or policy recommendation. I just think of that mustard seed slowly growing into a fruitful tree." He looked at Emily. "It's hard to be patient when you try so hard and want to make improvements so fast, but sometimes you just have to be a mustard seed." The next morning Sam placed an envelope of small seeds in Emily's purse with a note that read: "Tell me when these begin to sprout."

Assuming you have selected a recent, meaningful experience, have set aside adequate time, and are reflecting with suitable partners, what do you do next? How do you go about making faith-sense? In the following pages I propose a method with four steps. The steps can be easily remembered by the acronym NAME, as in, to name the faith-sense of your experience. The letters stand for Narration, Analysis, Meaning, and Enactment.

Narration

The first step in making faith-sense of your experience is to narrate it. This corresponds to the letter "N." It simply means telling what happened. You do not have to be a novelist or reporter to do this. In fact, if you are like most people, you already narrate your experiences because human beings are instinctive story tellers. "You won't believe what happened at work today," a husband says to his wife when he arrives home. "Wait till I tell you about our vacation," one neighbor says to another. "Let's have lunch and catch up on what's been happening," two friends agree who have not seen each other for a while. We even invite one another to narrate our experiences. "What happened at school today?" a parent asks her child. "How did your business trip go?" one office worker asks another.

SPEAKING AND WRITING

As these everyday examples indicate, the most natural form of narration is a verbal description. This is an account of events, more or less as they occurred, re-presented for your own reflection or for sharing with others (your partners). When I recall my friend who died recently, I do not think of his general qualities or professional achievements. I tell myself about the things we did together; I hear his favorite expressions and the way he would say, "Is that right?" whenever I would share a bit of news. When Paula returned from the grocery store, she surely did not speak in generalities about the plight of the elderly in our society. She undoubtedly described the man who bagged her groceries and told her husband about the impact his comment had on her.

Next to speaking, writing is the most natural way for people to narrate their experiences. Writing has a few advantages over speaking. First of all, writing is a more permanent record of what happened. If you go back to the stories used in this chapter, you will find that they are still there, just as they were when you first read them, whereas a story told in the course of a conversation may be difficult to recall later (unless it was tape recorded). This permanence factor can make a difference when you try to make faith-sense of your experience.

Writing can also be more focused than speaking. This is especially true if you take time to formulate your narration, selecting words and images carefully, even revising them to make the description more clear or accurate. A well-written account of an experience is a real asset in getting to its core meaning because it makes the experience easier to recall and analyze (the next step in the process of making faith-sense).

Finally, writing has its own dynamic, similar to the effect, mentioned above, of actually telling another person something you have been thinking about. Words have a power that is not completely controlled by the writer. Sometimes they suggest associations the writer is not fully conscious of. If Emily had been writing her thoughts about being promoted, the phrase "internal customer" might have triggered for her the same association with "charity begins at home" which it did for her friend. Sometimes words reveal things more sharply and unavoidably than the writer wants to acknowledge. If Henrietta were to write out her reactions to the school board's vote, she might see words like racism, failure, and wasted effort more starkly than she wants to deal with them.

The revealing power of the written word is one reason why people like to keep a journal. It not only helps them recall events and how they felt about them at the time; it also conveys meanings and implications which the journal writer did not have in mind. Re-reading your reflections can be like talking to another person, and a great aid in making faith-sense of your experience.

On the other hand, writing lacks the spontaneity and immediacy of telling someone your experience. There is a more human, natural quality to speaking and listening than there is to writing and reading. And unless you are a very good writer, it is hard to convey adequately the emotional quality of an important experience in a written narration. If Chuck and Eileen, or Henrietta, were to write a dispassionate, objective account of their situation, it would not be as helpful for making faith-sense as listening to them stagger around verbally while they express how they really feel about the events that have occurred in their lives. Of course, speaking and writing are not incompatible with each other and should not be put in opposition. They are the two most common ways people describe their experience and share it with others. You should feel free to choose whichever one works better for you, or fits a particular occasion better. In either case, the primary goal of narration is to describe your experience factually.

FACTUAL NARRATION

A factual narration is an account of events without any personal interpretation, i.e., without saying what you think the events mean or why people acted as they did. That part comes later. Initially you want to describe only what happened. Your description should certainly include how you felt about the event but not why you felt that way. For example, Henrietta had many emotional reactions to the school board's vote. In narrating this experience she should say that she was angry at the school board's action and concerned about its implications for the children. Her feelings are factual. However, it would go beyond a factual account for her to say that the members of the school board are racist or do not care about poor children. These are interpretations which require more than a statement of facts to be validated.

As you can imagine (and have probably experienced yourself), it is not always easy to stick to the facts and hold off interpreting them or attributing motives to people. This is especially difficult when you are emotionally affected by an experience. Partners can be a big help in this regard, but there is a more basic question to address. Why be so concerned about giving a strictly factual narration of your experience? There are two reasons.

First of all, making faith-sense begins with experiences which have their own meaning and value. In order that events may reveal this meaning on their own terms, you should let them speak for themselves before you add your interpretation. A factual narration accomplishes this.

For example, Chuck and Eileen may be eager to interpret Chuck's firing as a sign of what God is asking of them next.

However, a complete factual account of the experience might well reveal that Chuck was not really doing his job. He was so taken with the social mission of his company that he failed to run the business profitably enough to achieve the social mission. Instead of immediately interpreting this event as a new call from God, Chuck and Eileen may have to confront what the event itself is telling them: Chuck failed to do what was expected of him in the last job. Recognizing this, he may be better prepared to respond to what God is asking next.

Beginning with a factual account of experience and letting it reveal its own spiritual meaning on its own terms is a very incarnational approach to life. It puts into practice the belief that God truly became human and continues to come from within human experience. In this respect making faith-sense is an act of trust in God's prior presence and initiative (grace) in your life rather than assuming that you must supply the spiritual meaning for otherwise empty experiences. By attending to what actually happens before adding your own interpretation, you avoid acting spiritually self-sufficient and you let God have the first word by speaking through your experience.

This leads to the second reason for beginning with a factual narration of events. Everyone has opinions, personal convictions, points of view, preferences, and even prejudices. As events occur in your life, you will tend to see your positions verified, whether they are or not. You will look for objective evidence that you are right. Sometimes this can cause you to view things selectively, omitting what does not fit your preconceptions; sometimes it can lead you to rationalize or justify things artificially, making sense of them to yourself but not to anyone else. A factual account of events holds this tendency in check and keeps you accountable to reality as it actually occurs.

For example, Emily has been working hard to balance her family and career responsibilities. She is a strong advocate of each woman achieving her full potential and wants to make a contribution to that goal through her devotion to motherhood and dedication to her profession. She instinctively interpreted her promotion as a confirmation of her success in both areas.

What Emily overlooked was that her promotion enabled the Human Resources Department to meet its goal of "minority" placements for the year and thereby qualify for an incentive bonus. In addition, Emily was chosen over two men who were equally qualified, but one of them is not considered a team player because he expresses his disagreements in company meetings and the other is suspected of being gay. Moreover, because she has fewer years of service than either of the men, her salary is less than theirs would have been, which pleased the Vice President of Finance and swayed him to concur with her promotion. None of these facts negates the meaning Emily saw in her promotion, but they put her perception of things in a more realistic framework and keep her from formulating a one-sided, artificially spiritual explanation of events.

Facts can sometimes clobber your ideals and cherished wishes, but they can also bring you closer to the truth and that is the ultimate goal of making faith-sense. Hard as it might be to face reality and accommodate your desires to its demands, each time you do so you enter more deeply into the spirit of Jesus. He was very uncompromising, even to the point of being harsh, in measuring how well the facts corresponded to his ideals. More than once he chided the Twelve for their lack of faith and inability to grasp his teachings rather than pretend they were model followers.

He refused to placate religious leaders, even when they invited him to dinner, reprimanding his host on one occasion for not extending to him the usual courtesies (Luke 7:36-50), and challenging the guests on another occasion for maneuvering into seats of honor at table rather than accepting lower positions (Luke 14:7-14). He was not convinced that Peter would follow him to death just because he had appointed him head of the Twelve, and he was not misled by apparently sincere religious questions which were really intended to make him alienate some of his followers (Mark 12:13-27). For Jesus, as for anyone trying to make faith-sense, the facts are the foundation for constructing a spiritual interpretation.

The easiest way to give a factual account of any experience is to answer the basic questions: who? what? where? when? and how? You do not have to cover all these questions each time. They are a framework for focusing your attention on the event and the facts of the situation rather than your interpretation of it. There is another key question, of course, why? This question is so important that it has its own prominence as the second step of the method—analyzing the event—which will be discussed in the next section.

To illustrate the elements in a factual narration, consider the following example.

Cindy and her sister Ann were very close to each other when they were growing up in the 1950s. Their parents raised the children according to strict Christian principles and held high expectations for both of them. When Cindy decided to marry a divorced man, she knew her parents would not be pleased but she counted on Ann's support. To her shock, Ann told her that she, like her parents, would not attend the wedding and did not want to speak to her again.

Cindy believed that in time Ann's feelings would change. When she learned a few years later that Ann was engaged to be married, she tried to make contact with her but was told by relatives that she was not welcome as long as she was "living in sin." After that, Cindy was completely cut off from her sister and the rest of her family. She did not know where Ann lived, if she had children, or even if she was still alive. Just as painfully, she was unable to share her husband, her two children, and her first grandchild with Ann.

One day the phone rang and when Cindy answered it, she heard a long pause and then a hesitant voice, asking, "Aunt Cindy?" It was Frank, the eldest of Ann's three children. He explained that his mother had recently told them about Cindy, and he filled in a little information about their family. Then he said he was calling to tell her that his mother was very ill and to ask if she could come visit her. Cindy couldn't believe her ears. After nearly thirty years of silence and rejection, there was suddenly this invitation. She arranged to go immediately.

Cindy was both excited and fearful when she arrived at her sister's house. There were awkward introductions to the brother-in-law, nephew, and nieces she had never met.

There was an even more awkward reunion with her sister in her bedroom. Ann's weakness made it difficult for Cindy to express physically what she was feeling, but they were able to spend time talking together.

Cindy could not help but notice that on the wall over Ann's bed was a single framed photograph of the two of them, taken when they were teenagers. The photo prompted them to reminisce and begin catching up on what had been going on in their lives since they broke off communication. Eventually they talked about Ann's illness and her prospects for recovery, and they promised to stay in close contact in the future.

If Cindy wanted to make faith-sense of this experience, her first step would be to narrate it factually (as in the account just given). This means answering the basic information questions listed above.

1. *Who was involved?* This refers to the principal players in the event as well as those who were affected by it. Certainly Cindy and Ann are the primary players, but their parents and Cindy's husband also play a major role in the story. Both of their families have been affected by the thirty-year estrangement, highlighted by the fact that Frank made a hesitant phone call to an aunt he only recently learned about.

Is anyone else involved in this story, as you heard it? With whom do you find yourself identifying most closely?

2. *What happened?* This refers to the specific activities that constituted the event and gave it its significance. It is not a simple chronology of everything that took place, told with objective neutrality. It is a highlighting of those parts of the experience which hold the most meaning for you. It is not yet saying what that meaning is (this comes in stage three); it is saying that among all the things that happened, these are the ones which seem to call for making faith-sense.

Perhaps it was Cindy and Ann's childhood relationship, Cindy's marriage, her experience of being cut off from the family, Ann's illness, Frank's phone call, the sisters' reunion, the possibility of new, more satisfying family relationships. Any of these elements may strike you because you have experienced something similar in your life or you know someone who has.

As you think about the events which constitute this story, which ones stand out for you? What happened that would invite you to make faith-sense of it?

3. *Where did the events take place?* In an obvious sense this refers to the physical location where things happened; in a faith sense it also refers to the symbolic value of the setting. The primary location in the story is Ann's home, which suggests the meaning of a homecoming or family reunion. The photo of Cindy and Ann in the bedroom has a special poignancy, symbolizing that Ann kept Cindy close to her even though they were not in communication.

As you think about where this incident took place, is there anything else that stands out in your mind? What is the symbolic value of the setting to you?

4. *When did the events occur?* As with the location, this refers not only to the actual time period during which events took place but also to any significance that time period might have. The primary time period is the thirty-year gap in Cindy and Ann's relationship. Prior to that was the time they spent together growing up. There is also the timing of Ann's illness and a future which is suddenly real, complicated, and uncertain.

As you consider when this story occurred, what significance does it have for you and what does it suggest about its meaning from a faith perspective?

5. *How did events unfold?* This question refers to the sequence of events, how one thing led to or followed another, and what their cumulative impact was on the participants and others, like yourself, who may only have observed and heard about them. There are two sequences in this story. The first is Cindy and Ann's childhood, Cindy's marriage, and her subsequent isolation from the family; the second is Ann's telling her children about Cindy, Frank's phone call, and the subsequent reunion. The impact of the first sequence is exactly reversed in the second, with the experience of family running throughout.

As you consider how the events of this story unfolded, what connections do you see? How did events before and after contribute to its meaning?

EXERCISE

There are two goals to achieve in narrating an experience. The first is to represent it as accurately and completely as possible. This helps to achieve the second goal, which is to let the experience reveal its own meaning on its own terms. Both goals are facilitated by a reasonably complete factual account.

To sharpen your ability to describe an experience, return to the one you selected on page 15 (or choose a different experience if you prefer). Now ask:

1. Who was involved? (the principal players and others affected by the experience, including yourself)
2. What happened? (the main events and their significance)
3. Where did it happen? (the location and its symbolic value)
4. When did it happen? (the time period and its symbolic value)
5. How did it happen? (the sequence of events and their impact on you).

Are your answers factual? Have you narrated the event without inserting judgments about people's motives or an interpretation of what the event might mean? With an accurate, factual description, you are ready for the next step in the method—analysis.

Analysis

A relatively complete factual narration is the foundation for analyzing an experience—the second step in the method of making faith-sense, corresponding to the letter "A" in the acronym NAME. When you analyze an experience, you uncover the reasons why it occurred as it did. This is actually an extension of your factual description, except that now you examine the facts themselves to gain a clearer and more accurate understanding of them.

The key question in analyzing an experience is, why? Why would Cindy's decision to marry a divorced man cause such a complete and uncompromising break with Ann, especially if they had been so close growing up? Was someone else involved? If so, why did that person have such influence? Why were efforts not made to overcome this alienation at some point during those thirty years? Why did the initiative come at this particular time and why did it come through a nephew whom Cindy had never met? Are there other "why" questions about this event which occur to you?

In response to the why questions Cindy asked, Ann told her that she never really wanted to be cut off from her. She did not care that Cindy's husband was divorced, as long as they loved one another and Cindy was happy. It was Ann's father who forced her to stay away from Cindy. Ann did not want to offend her father at the time because she feared he would take it out on her mother.

Then after several years without contact, she concluded that Cindy wanted nothing to do with her. That thought pained her even more than their separation, but she understood why Cindy would feel this way. When her illness was discovered, Ann told her children for the first time that they had an aunt and that she and Cindy had not been in contact all these years. Frank, sensing his mother's desire to see Cindy, got busy and tracked her down. Analyzing a narrative with why questions often helps to uncover additional facts as well as lead to an explanation of the facts already known.

The most effective way to analyze a narrative is to apply the why question to the categories of information used in narrating the experience. *Who* else was involved that might explain why things happened as they did? The father. *What happened?* Ann did not want to offend her father and wanted to protect her mother; her actions were not really aimed at Cindy and did not represent her true feelings about Cindy. Does the *place* or *time* period suggest why things happened as they did? A family setting governed by strict moral principles and a domineering father in the late 1950s might help to explain why Ann agreed to break off contact with Cindy and why she never tried to restore it. *How* did the breakthrough occur; what was the sequence of events which explains why the current experience took place? Ann's illness was the occasion for the change although she did not initiate the action herself. Instead she revealed a few facts to her children and relied on them to follow through, almost as if she were asking them to mediate or redeem her relationship with Cindy.

Answers to the why questions can begin to sketch the faith-sense which this event might have. The father's strict moral outlook recalls the cautions in both the Jewish and Christian Scriptures about a rigid, legalistic mentality that can be harmful to persons and displeasing to God (Matthew 23). The thirty-year gap in Cindy and Ann's relationship parallels the periods of exile when the Jews were separated from their homeland as well as the hidden life of Jesus before he began his public ministry. The reunion of the sisters invokes the themes of mediation, forgiveness, reconciliation, and even redemption. The experience of their coming together, telling their stories, and celebrating their lives has liturgical overtones which may be ritualized either within their own families or by publicly worshipping together at church. Are there other associations from the faith tradition which this analysis suggests to you?

As this example indicates, the answers to the why questions are not hidden in a mysterious divine plan. In order to make faith-sense of her experience, Cindy does not have to think that God wanted her and Ann to be separated all those years or that their reunion is God's way of helping Ann deal with her illness. An analysis of experience seeks factual answers (Ann gave in to an overbearing father; she and Cindy enjoy being back together again regardless of Ann's health). Analysis trusts that these deeper facts will provide the basis for making faith-sense, but it does not assume that these answers are self-evident. A little probing and testing are required to uncover them.

On the other hand, the probing questions of analysis do not mean you should always be suspicious, much less skeptical, about the reasons people give for why things happen. Analyzing experience for the sake of making faith-sense is not the same as analyzing a person's unconscious for the sake of psychotherapy. Cindy does not have to keep asking Ann: "Is that *really* why you didn't contact me all those years? Is that *really* why you complied with what dad wanted?"

The purpose of analyzing an experience for faith-sense is to enter it with greater attentiveness and to let the experience reveal all that it has to offer. A well-analyzed experience is the best basis for making faith-sense because it provides a true-to-life standard for the spiritual or theological meaning you may claim. This is not to restrict faith-sense but to keep it real, practical, and livable.

For example, if Cindy and Ann were to make faith-sense of their experience based on the further analysis of why they became distanced in the first place, they would realize that it was an unfortunate and unintended separation which they cannot go back and undo. However, they can begin to create a new relationship. In doing so, they are living out the call of Jesus found everywhere in the gospels to recognize the signs of God's life in the present moment and respond to them. Frank's phone call is such a sign, and Cindy's recognition of this and response to it enables her to begin making faith-sense of it. She is not just responding to her nephew or her sister; she is also responding to the Lord living in their midst, who for the last thirty years has remained in the gaps in their relationship, in their silence and absence, waiting to bring them back together.

This last point might remind Cindy of the story of Jesus and Lazarus. As John tells it (11:1-44), Lazarus was near death and his sisters, Martha and Mary, sent word to Jesus, but he did not come right away. In the meantime Lazarus died. Jesus' delay puzzled and disturbed the sisters who wanted to know why he did not come sooner and they speculated about what might have happened if he had. Jesus did not take that approach. He did not give them an explanation for his delay but rather he reaffirmed their faith in the new life of resurrection and then he enacted it by raising Lazarus from death.

Cindy and Ann could easily dwell on the past and relive the hurt, confusion, and anger that filled it. In that case they would be like Lazarus lying in the tomb and the sisters complaining to Jesus about his absence. But they could also see their situation as an invitation to reaffirm the newness of life and to act on it by beginning to reconstruct their relationship. In that case they would be like Lazarus coming forth from the tomb and sitting down at table with Jesus once more (as John narrates in chapter 12:1-2). In this way Cindy and Ann would be making faith-sense not just in thought but in deed.

Are there other parallels you see in the story of Jesus and Lazarus? Can you think of other biblical stories or signs of God's presence which might make better faith-sense of this incident?

EXERCISE

To sharpen your skill in analyzing an experience, return to the event you have already selected and described above (or choose and describe a different experience). Now ask:

1. Why were these people involved?
2. Why did things happen the way they did?
3. Why was the situation structured the way it was?
4. Why did things happen at this time?
5. Why did this sequence of events occur, one thing leading to another?

Having narrated and analyzed an experience that is meaningful in your life, you are now ready to explore its faith meaning, to make sense of it from a faith perspective. Although this is part of a continuous process, it will be discussed in a separate chapter because of its importance.

CHAPTER THREE

How to Make Faith-Sense: The Heart of the Matter

The heart of making faith-sense is to determine the spiritual meaning of the event you are reflecting on. This is the third step in the method being presented here, and it corresponds to the letter "M" in the acronym, NAME. It is where a factual account of experience (step one) and a deeper analysis of the facts (step two) meet the values and lessons contained in the faith tradition.

But suppose you feel you do not have much knowledge about your faith tradition. Perhaps you have never formally studied the Bible or taken a course in theology. Maybe your acquaintance with the faith is based on Sunday school instructions, listening to sermons, observing Christian behavior, and bits and pieces of information you pick up from conversations and news reports. If so, you are like numerous other believers—and you are ready to make faith-sense.

Making faith-sense does not require a degree in theology. All that faith-sense requires is that you bring whatever knowledge and experience of the faith you have and remain open to additional learning. Furthermore, a formal, academic understanding of theology is not the same as making faith-sense. Formal theology is a summary of a vast body of experience and reflection, condensed into a few general ideas that are arranged in a coherent, systematic order. This is a marvelous resource for quick, efficient learning, but it is not the way life occurs or the way theological meaning appears in everyday experience. If you are expecting formal, systematic theology in the experiences you make faith-sense of, you probably will not find it.

It is important to remember that in making faith-sense, there are no predetermined, correct answers. Making faith-sense is not like working a crossword puzzle. It is a personal, creative undertaking which draws upon the accumulated wisdom and experience of the faith tradition. This allows plenty of room for variety and different viewpoints. In listening to the story of Cindy and Ann in the previous chapter, I may focus on their opportunity to create a new relationship; you may focus on the need for forgiveness and reconciliation. I may see parallels in the story of Jesus and Lazarus; you may see parallels in different biblical stories.

Of course, there are some conclusions and interpretations which are not consistent with the meaning of Christianity. If in a spirit of vindictiveness Cindy refused to see Ann at all or in a spirit of self-righteousness insisted that Ann come to her, her faith-sense would not be in harmony with the values of Christianity no matter how she felt personally. In this respect, as with expanding your knowledge of the faith and seeing alternative points of view, partners are a valuable asset. They can make suggestions, offer perspectives, and indicate inconsistencies or shortcomings in your thinking that you might not have recognized by yourself.

With or without partners, however, making faith-sense is a creative and often challenging task that should also be stimulating and enlivening. This is more likely to be the case if the experience you select for reflection is engaging and important to you, because that experience is not only the starting point but also the guide to your more explicit theological reflection. To move into this phase, it is helpful, as you review your narration of the event and your analysis of it, to identify the one place where you felt most engaged. The information questions (who? what? where? when? and how?) provide a framework for doing this.

For example, in the story of Cindy and Ann you may have been drawn to the people in the story (who): to Cindy, her sister, their father, or Frank. You may have connected with the experience of their separation, or their reunion, or their future relationship (the "what" of the incident). You may have been moved by the idea of Ann's home as the site of their reunion or the photo of the sisters on her bedroom wall (where). You may have identified with the years of their childhood or the thirty years of their separation (when). You may have been struck by Ann's finally telling her children about their aunt, which led to Frank's phone call and Cindy's visit (how). Your analysis (why) may have put you in touch with how easily misunderstandings and lack of communication can disrupt relationships, or what it is like to be caught in a dilemma as Ann was, or how genuine love can overcome hurt and rejection to begin life anew.

Wherever your feelings lead you, that is where you are being drawn to make faith-sense. As you explore the meaning of your experience, you may make faith-sense of it in one of three ways: as an illustration which allows you to affirm what you believe; as a question or challenge which prompts you to adapt what you believe; as an insight which leads you to convert what you believe into something new. Each of these possibilities will be discussed in detail.

Affirmation

Most people make faith-sense of the events in their lives by interpreting them as an affirmation or illustration of what they already believe. This is to be expected. Christianity embraces the whole of life and Christians are taught to look at all aspects of life from a faith perspective. If you make decisions, structure your actions, and respond to events in terms of this encompassing faith orientation, you should expect to find your beliefs verified by your experience.

Spouses who love and care for each other rightly interpret their mutual acts of kindness, thoughtfulness, sensitivity, and self-giving as a concrete embodiment of what marriage means from a Christian perspective. Parents who raise their children to care for others, develop their own potential, and contribute to society should interpret their children's growth and accomplishments as a confirmation of their Christian parenthood. Workers who do the job they are hired to do, treat co-workers and customers with respect, and conduct themselves in a spirit of fairness, truth, and integrity can interpret their career advances and financial security as an affirmation of their Christian values in the workplace.

The same is true even when things do not work out as expected. Spouses who face problems in their marriage, possibly even divorce, will acknowledge that no one is perfect, both partners have to work together to make a marriage succeed, good intentions are no guarantee of success—all sentiments contained within the faith tradition and now confirmed by their concrete experience. Parents whose children get into trouble or adopt a value system different from theirs will recall that each person is a unique individual, that parenting does not mean controlling or cloning, that at some point all they can do is offer support and prayer—also sentiments found in the faith tradition. Workers who are treated unfairly, passed over for promotions, or whose companies move away, putting them out of work, will remind themselves that material prosperity is not what ultimately counts and that God's justice will triumph in the end.

This form of faith-sense is a reminder that, as a believer, you are not alone. Your ancestors in the faith have faced situations similar to yours in their lives. Their attempts at making faith-sense have become part of the faith tradition itself and are often handed down in phrases, maxims, and slogans similar to those just mentioned. This is all some people need to make faith-sense of their lives. However, if you want to explore your experience more fully and derive from it the fullest faith-meaning it can offer, then you will push beyond familiar affirmations and ask a different question: what does this experience remind me of in the faith tradition?

When an experience reminds you of a story, teaching, or practice from your faith tradition, it illustrates what you believe and helps you make faith-sense of that experience. For example, a few years ago I was invited to be part of an all-day planning group in an inner city parish. We broke for dinner and went to a nearby restaurant which was within walking distance of the church. On the way back from dinner, we were clustered in groups of two and three. About a block from the church we came upon a man lying on his side at the corner of a convenience store. He appeared to be either drunk or on drugs and was shabbily dressed. The first group, led by the pastor, walked by the man. The second group, of which I was a member, commented about the man but continued walking. Then we heard a couple of the women in the group behind us addressing the man. "Are you all right?" they asked. "Do you need any help?" We stopped and looked back. One of the women had stooped down to talk to the man who was slowly responding. Another woman had gone inside the store to call for help. As it turned out, the man was diabetic and had simply fainted.

When we reassembled, we postponed our planning session to reflect on this experience. Needless to say, the incident reminded everyone of the parable of the Good Samaritan. Those of us who passed by the man could not avoid comparing ourselves with the priest and Levite who did the same in Jesus' parable. On the other hand, the women who stopped to help did not think of themselves as good Samaritans or even as consciously putting their faith into practice. In their own words, they were just trying to be helpful. In the words of the gospel, however, they were being neighbors to the man and had "gone and done likewise," just as Jesus recommended.

Most experiences do not resemble a story or incident from the faith tradition as exactly as this one did. They are more like analogies where one or another aspect of the experience is similar to certain aspects of the faith tradition. This is where it helps to pay attention to the who, what, where, when, and how questions. They can provide the basis for analogies that illustrate the faith-sense of your experience. For example, Steve is a highway construction worker who recently made a retreat on the theme of Work and Spirituality. The retreatants were asked to relate the type of work they do to a spiritual value or theme—in effect, to make faith-sense of their work as a whole.

Steve said he identified with the passage from Isaiah, read at the liturgy during the Advent season, in which the prophet is told, "Prepare the way of the Lord; in the desert make straight his paths" (Mark 1:3; Isa 40:3). Steve hastened to assure the others that he did not think of himself as a real prophet like Isaiah, but he did often make a path in areas where there was none, sometimes literally in a desert. More importantly, he hoped that his work linked people together and gave them easier access to resources they need in their everyday lives. If so, he felt he was doing the work of the Lord.

In further conversation Steve also indicated that he was very conscious of using taxpayers' money and he felt a real obligation to complete projects on time. "Of course, we're pretty dependent on the weather," he said. "In that respect we're a lot like farmers, except that good weather for them is bad weather for us, and vice versa."

In his comments Steve drew an analogy between himself and the prophet Isaiah (who), and between his work in areas where there were no roads and the prophet's work of making a path in the desert for the Lord (where). He also affirmed the value of timely completion of his work (when) and dependence on the weather (how) and hoped that his roads might link people and make their lives better (what). Not everything about Steve's job fit the call of the prophet Isaiah but there were enough similarities for him to make faith-sense of his work by affirming it as an illustration of his beliefs.

Of course, some experiences are neither a perfect fit nor a good analogy but the exact opposite. They express attitudes and values that are inconsistent with Christian beliefs, if they are not outright contradictions. The most blatant examples are incidents of racism, sexism, bigotry, greed, violence and the like, but there are also more subtle distortions of Christian values which may not be as easily recognized. The world of advertising produces the most numerous examples of this.

Advertisements are a major part of the popular culture. They not only promote products or services, they also express values and portray behavior that may actually be contrary to Christian values, even if they are presented in a humorous or entertaining way. For example, there is a beer commercial on television in which four young men are climbing a mountain. Two of them reach the top where a six-pack is nestled in the snow, just where they had left it. The two men on the ground shout up, asking if the beer is still there. The two at the top look at each other, communicating silently, and then yell back down, "No."

The obvious intent of the commercial is to tell how good this beer is. But the message is conveyed in a way that encourages selfishness (the two "at the top" keep the beer for themselves rather than share it with their friends farther down the mountain). Furthermore, the ad condones lying for the sake of selfish pursuits. In these ways the commercial contradicts Christian values, and the only way to make faith-sense of it is to affirm the opposite.

Whenever an experience reminds you of a biblical story (like the Good Samaritan), suggests analogies with a religious figure (like the prophet Isaiah), or even contradicts your Christian values (like the beer commercial), it is inviting you to make faith-sense of it as an illustration of what you believe. To do this, you need to recall what you already know from your faith tradition and be ready to draw upon additional sources which are relevant to the experience. In general the most common sources of the faith for doing this are Scripture, history, doctrine, morality, and worship.

1. *Scripture* is the first and most common source which is illustrated by everyday experience. First of all, the Bible is the basis for other forms of religious expression in Christianity. As the revealed Word of God, it is the foundation on which everything else rests. Second, most people are more familiar with the Bible than with other sources of the faith such as history or doctrine. Their experiences remind them of Bible stories and passages more readily than anything else, even if they do not know exactly where to find certain incidents in the Bible. Third, and more directly related to making faith-sense, the Bible is full of religious stories and narratives. Its literary form is closer to the way people experience and express events in their lives than any other source of the faith. For all these reasons most of the examples used so far in this book have a biblical parallel.

2. *History* is a source of faith-sense as a continuation and extension of the stories of faith in Scripture. While it is important to know who did what, when things happened, and how one event led to the emergence of another, the real value of history for making faith-sense is the example of countless people who have concretized the Christian way of life in their own circumstances. Their stories, struggles, and achievements provide a script which can help you as a contemporary believer locate yourself and make faith-sense of your experience. For example, the sixteenth-century Mexican peasant, Juan Diego, has inspired generations of Mexicans to see themselves not as rejected, marginal

people but as privileged bearers of God's good news communicated to them through Juan Diego's vision of the Lady of Guadalupe.

3. Concrete experiences often illustrate *doctrines* of the faith, not in their precise, carefully worded, and officially approved form but as broad themes of Christian belief. The examples used thus far have illustrated the doctrinal themes of birth and friendship (Michelle and her family), failure and recommitment (Chuck and Eileen), aging and human dignity (Paula and the grocery store man), grief and memory (my friend who died), equality and concern for the poor (Henrietta and the school board), business practices and charity (Emily and her promotion), forgiveness and reconciliation (Cindy and Ann), compassion and service (the women who helped the diabetic), work as a vocation and help to others (Steve, the highway man). Each of these themes in the faith tradition probably contains more information than you need to make faith-sense of a specific incident, but the incidents themselves draw attention to the themes and illustrate their relevance in everyday life.

4. When a concrete experience calls for a decision and leads to direct action as a result, it illustrates the faith source of *morality*. This source is handed on in the form of moral principles as well as examples of moral behavior. The everyday experiences which illustrate the moral tradition of Christianity most frequently occur in the context of work, sexual behavior, and health care. Most business decisions have moral implications, ranging from the treatment of employees, the use of natural resources and the disposal of waste, truth in advertising, respect for customers, responding to competitors, making a profit, and contributing to the common good.

Sexual activity illustrates moral teaching about the nature and purpose of sexuality, the dignity and rights of women, men, and children, the issues of birth control, abortion, and sterilization as well as artificial insemination and in vitro fertilization. Health care and medical practice illustrate the moral perspective on the human body, the quality of life, the justification of risk and experiment, the allocation of resources, the relative value of physical life and its relation to belief in life everlasting. The situations in these areas often pose challenging questions to the faith tradition, which leads to the second way of making faith-sense to be described below. However, they also illustrate the moral values and recall the examples of moral living which are part of the faith tradition and can help make faith-sense of your decisions and actions.

5. *Worship* is a central experience of the Christian life that makes use of symbols and rituals to express the belief of Christian people. Some traditions are more elaborate than others in their use of material symbols and formal rituals; certain traditions may highlight one aspect (vestments, symbolic gestures, ancient prayers) more than another (congregational participation, preaching, spontaneous prayer), but all Christian worship ritualizes life. For this reason the everyday rituals and symbols in people's experience can illustrate and affirm the liturgical expression of their faith.

For example, the customs you develop with your spouse to express your love and commitment to each other can also be a reminder of Christ's love for you as members of the Church, as St. Paul suggested long ago in his letter to the Ephesians (5:21-33). The way you instruct and feed your children, and celebrate events with them, can be a reminder of the Liturgy of the Word and Eucharist (as the description of the family as a "domestic church" suggests). Your care for the environment through recycling, avoiding throw-away products, and enhancing beauty recalls how the liturgy treats the material world with respect and reverence. In all these ways you can make faith-sense of your everyday experience as an illustration of the worship tradition of the Church.

In determining which faith sources are most appropriate to your experience, you may find it helpful to pay attention to the information question in your narration which appeals to you the most. This provides an initial orientation to the faith tradition because each question corresponds in a general way to one of the faith sources. "Who" usually suggests biblical or historical figures (the women who stopped to help the diabetic man illustrated the good Samaritan). "What" lends itself to doctrinal themes and moral principles (the women's action recalled the doctrines of charity and neighborliness as well as the moral precept to help the suffering). "Where" often invokes worship in the sense of sacred space, the place where God is present and honored (the street outside the convenience store was typical of the public places where Jesus healed and fed people as a sign of true worship). "When" relates to history (the women's action, and the neglect by the rest of us, are part of a long and continuing history of reactions to the needs of others). "How" refers to moral behavior and liturgical action (the women responded with appropriate action, and their action provided comfort and healing for the man).

It is important to keep in mind, however, that these questions provide only an initial orientation; they do not exhaust the possibilities for making faith-sense. In fact, they may not even prove to be the most fruitful connections. You do not necessarily make your best faith-sense on the first try or by settling for the first association that comes to mind. For example, Steve had already drawn a biblical parallel between his work of highway construction and the passage in Isaiah which is read at the liturgy during Advent. In conversation with others on the retreat, he was encouraged to see his work itself as a kind of liturgy, glorifying God by incorporating the moral values of truth through the quality and integrity of his work, and of life through his treatment of co-workers and benefits to the public. This proved to be a richer affirmation of Steve's faith than his own initial reflection.

In order to make the best faith-sense of your experience as an affirmation of what you believe, you may want to list all the connections that come to mind. If you are sharing this experience with partners, add their suggestions to the list. Select the one reference that holds the most promise or interest for you, and begin to explore it. If it is a biblical story, look it up and re-read it, noting similarities and differences with your situation (e.g., the parable of the Good Samaritan is in Luke 10:30-37). If your experience illustrates a historical event or person, find out what you can about it by asking your pastor or a parish staff person, or consult a religious encyclopedia (e.g., what was Isaiah's situation when God asked him to make a path through the desert?). If you are reminded of a doctrinal theme or moral principle, like charity or neighborliness, you might check it in a catechism or reference book which may lead you to additional topics such as the corporal works of mercy or the relationship between charity and justice. If your experience suggests a parallel with liturgical practice, you could pay closer attention to it the next time you worship. In these ways you not only use what you and your partners already know, but you let your experience broaden your knowledge of the faith.

BENEFITS

When you make faith-sense of an experience as an affirmation of your beliefs, you are not just carrying out an intellectual exercise or reinforcing the status quo. It is true that an illustration affirms what you already know and believe, but it does more than that. It confirms your faith and reassures you of its relevance by showing you in concrete, everyday terms that what you believe is real and relevant to your life. An affirmation matches abstract ideas and general beliefs with personal, lived experience, and offers you greater confidence in shaping your life and taking action according to your religious beliefs. I for one am more likely to stop and help someone in need because my experience illustrated the parable of the Good Samaritan.

An affirmation also provides concrete examples that help you recognize the reality of your faith as it appears in the circumstances of your life. The more you practice the skill of making faith-sense, the more you recognize your beliefs in the day-to-day events of your life. As a result, your faith and the rest of your life become more integrated. You do not have to act one way in church and a different way in society.

CAUTION

The biggest caution about seeing your experience as an affirmation of your faith is that you can begin to impose religious meaning artificially on your experience or feel that every event should have a deep spiritual significance. A person who holds the door for you out of politeness is not necessarily an example of Christian servanthood; a co-worker who habitually says "God bless you" when you sneeze is not necessarily an illustration of bringing God into the workplace.

Partners can help keep you honest in this respect but even if you reflect on your experience privately, you should always try to let your experience be your guide. There is no need to force what is not there. Making faith-sense is a personal and creative act but it is not "make-believe" or pretense. It is letting your experience illustrate your faith and letting your faith illuminate your experience. Asking the information questions, looking for examples, analogies, or even contradictions, and reviewing the major sources of the faith tradition are all aids in a natural, realistic process. The faith-meaning that your experience actually illustrates is more than ample; you do not have to contrive anything to make it work.

EXAMPLE

To concretize further how experience can affirm and illustrate your faith, consider the following example.

Pam was recently hired as a telephone receptionist for a national phone order company. The pay is good and the hours are flexible, but she works in a room with thirty others, all in cubicles, answering phones and either processing orders or handling complaints. Pam feels like a robot, confined to her cubicle, talking to strangers all day, trying to be enthusiastic about their orders, and pretending to be interested in why one customer is ordering this style of bed linen and that customer is returning an ironing board cover.

During one of their breaks, a co-worker, Sandy, asked Pam if she was coming to The Cubicle Crew's luncheon next week. "What's that?" Pam wanted to know. Sandy explained that once a month about a half dozen of the receptionists sponsor a fund-raising event for someone in need. The event is held during the lunch hour on the grounds surrounding the building where they work. "Usually it's a pot luck lunch," Sandy said, "but we've also had a pie-eating contest, ethnic food celebration, and even a celebrity look-alike show."

Everyone who works for the company (about one hundred fifty) is invited and asked to pay $5.00 admission.

All the money is given to the individual or group chosen for that month. Recommendations are made by any employee and then The Cubicle Crew makes the selection. The recipients are also invited, but they are not expected to say or do anything. "We don't want to exploit them or force them to thank us," Sandy explained. "We just want to meet them so we can get to know them a little bit—and get to know one another better. Sometimes I think that's the real benefit of these fund raisers. They get us out of our cubicles and into one another's lives."

Pam readily agreed to come to the "Tempting Tacos" lunch. On the day of the event, she was surprised at how many of her co-workers participated. It gave her a chance to meet many of them for the first time and to become better acquainted with those she had seen around the building. Best of all, she spent time with the family who received the proceeds from the event.

Afterwards, Pam asked Sandy how the whole project got started. Sandy told her that about a year ago one of their co-workers had a terrible fire that destroyed her apartment and most of her possessions. Fortunately she and her two children were unharmed. "We all wanted to do something, so we took up a collection and the response was truly amazing. Some of us talked about it afterward and concluded that most people really do want to help those in need, especially if we personally know them. From that experience The Cubicle Crew was born."

This is a factual narration of Pam's experience. It identifies persons involved (Pam, Sandy, The Cubicle Crew, co-workers, people in need). It describes the work Pam does, how it affects her, the invitation from Sandy, her participation in the lunch, and the impact it made on her. It mentions where and when these events take place (at the work site during the lunch hour once a month) and explains how the recipients are chosen and who organizes the event (The Cubicle Crew). Pam's question about how this practice began also leads to a little further analysis concerning the reason why the recipients are invited (for personal contact) and the value of these lunches for the employees (to get them into each other's lives). Any of these points could provide an entry for Pam if she wants to reflect on this experience and make faith-sense of it, by herself or with others, possibly even with The Cubicle Crew.

The first way Pam could do this is to ask if it affirms or illustrates what she already believes. She might recall, for example, the general Christian doctrine of love for others, especially the poor and those in need. Charity, in this sense, is the hallmark of Christian living and the heart of Christian morality. A further expression of this charity is helping others in a way that respects them as persons and preserves their dignity. The fund raisers of The Cubicle Crew seem to affirm these doctrinal and moral teachings and allow Pam to make sense of the experience as an illustration of her faith. Do other doctrinal themes or moral principles occur to you in this event?

Pam might also refer to numerous biblical passages ranging from the Mosaic precept to treat the stranger with hospitality (Lev 19:33-34) to Elisha helping a widow besieged by creditors (2 Kgs 4:1-7) to Jesus' feeding of the multitude (Luke 9:10-17). Historical examples also abound, including the stories of individual saints like St. Francis of Assisi, the establishment of Church agencies and organizations to serve the poor, and contemporary examples such as the good works of Mother Teresa of Calcutta. Do other biblical or historical examples come to your mind?

However, it was not until Pam attended church the following Sunday that the deepest meaning of her experience became clear to her. As she participated in the liturgy, she was reminded of the taco lunch. Like the Lord's supper, it brought everyone together on an equal level and made them a community. Each person shared what others provided and they all became better acquainted through the experience. When she received communion during the liturgy, it was both an extension and completion of her experience from earlier that week. Do any other liturgical parallels occur to you?

If Pam wanted to explore these connections further, she could read and meditate on the suggested biblical parallels, study the lives of some outstanding examples of Christian charity, review the theological meaning of concern for the needy, or consider the social dimension of Christian worship. In short, her experience could continue to affirm and illustrate her faith in many ways for a long time. That is what it means to make faith-sense.

EXERCISE

The first and most common way of making faith-sense is to affirm your faith by letting your experience illustrate what you believe. To practice this form of making faith-sense, go back to the experience you selected earlier, or choose a different one, and ask the following questions:

1. Does this experience remind me of anything in the faith tradition? Is it an exact parallel or reenactment, an analogy, or a contradiction of what I know and believe?
2. How many illustrations does this experience suggest? Which one do I want to focus on?
3. Which sources of the faith does this experience illustrate: Scripture, history, doctrine, morality, worship?
4. How can I explore these sources more fully: look up biblical passages, consult reference books, talk with knowledgeable people?
5. As I make faith-sense of this experience with the help of the sources of faith, how does it affect me? Do I have greater confidence in living my faith, better facility in recognizing my beliefs in daily events? Does my interpretation seem consistent with the experience itself or am I forcing it in any way?

Adaptation

Sometimes an experience does not confirm your faith so much as confront it with questions and challenges. Pam's experience could also make her ask: why do the people helped by The Cubicle Crew suffer in the first place? Why do we always have the poor with us (as Jesus predicted)? Are Christians more concerned about themselves than those in need?

When these kinds of questions arise, they require more than an affirmation of what you already believe. They call your faith into question and challenge you to affirm it differently. Instead of reminding you of what you know and believe, they make you rethink it and adapt it to make faith-sense of the experience confronting you.

Experiences of this type are different from analogies or outright contradictions, which were noted in the previous section. Analogies and contradictions lead to affirmations of the faith as you know and live it; challenging experiences push beyond the status quo of your faith-sense and make you wrestle with your beliefs in order to make sense of your experience. The persistent emphasis is "yes, but," and the constant question is "why."

Everyone is mortal, but why should a child be born with HIV contracted from a mother who was raped by a drug addict? Adolescence is a troubling and volatile period of life, but why does a teenager open fire on classmates, killing several of them? Clergy are ministers of the gospel in whom people place their trust and confidence, but why do some of them take advantage of their position and sexually abuse children?

Negative and traumatic experiences like these are the clearest examples of challenges to the faith, but sometimes positive experiences can have the same effect on those who want to make faith-sense. Jim, a talented business manager with twenty years of experience, was recently promoted to a position with a higher salary than he ever dreamed of, but he finds the work not very stimulating and feels underutilized. The career advancement and financial security are welcome developments but they make him question the value and purpose of his work from a personal and faith perspective.

Ginny, the youngest of three children, leaves home for college, and for the first time in twenty-five years her parents can turn their attention to themselves. They enjoy the freedom from parental responsibility and the chance to "reward" themselves for their years of dedication and sacrifice, but they also wonder whether they should be using more of their new-found time and resources to help others. Culturally, the Internet is a remarkable development with unknown possibilities for communication and efficiency, but it has already raised questions about the exposure of children to adult material and the increased isolation of individuals who interact electronically but do not necessarily interrelate personally.

To make faith-sense of experiences like these, take the same approach as above. First, narrate the events and then analyze them. Any of the factual elements you identify might raise the question that calls for an adaptation of your belief, although it is more likely that the analysis question—why—will provide this stimulus.

For example, when Martin Luther King Jr. began to lead non-violent protests and organize boycotts which included civil disobedience, many devout Christians were shocked and scandalized. They had learned to respect and obey the law and value public order. The actions of Dr. King challenged their faith in many respects. First of all, he was a minister of the gospel (who). Second, he was deliberately breaking the law and promoting civil disobedience (what). Third, he did so in public and, for some, in their own communities (where) at a time (when) of relative prosperity for most Americans. Finally, he employed tactics of non-violent confrontation and resistance (how) which seemed to provoke violent reactions from citizens and law officers and cause physical suffering for demonstrators.

All these facts posed challenging questions for people of faith, but the most disturbing questions came from a further analysis of why Dr. King was practicing civil disobedience. The laws he broke were unjust laws. His non-violent resistance exposed the injustice of legalized segregation and confronted Christians with the fact that their respect for the law may have been no more than blind obedience which actually perpetuated injustice. It was also possible, of course, that Christians who upheld discriminatory laws were actually racists, but that was a different question which each person had to face in conscience. An analysis of the facts alone meant that Christians had to examine their belief in law and order; they had to clarify that only just laws required obedience whereas unjust laws had to be changed, perhaps through the very means of civil disobedience and non-violent resistance.

When an experience like this calls for an adaptation of your belief in order to make faith-sense of it, there are at least three ways you can proceed.

MODIFY YOUR UNDERSTANDING

The first and most common way of adapting your belief is to modify your understanding of it. A good example of this in the New Testament is provided by St. Paul. The first Christians, probably including Paul himself, believed that Jesus would return in their lifetime to consummate the history of the world and reward those who had been faithful to him. However, when some of the disciples began to die before these concluding events took place, the rest were troubled and began to question whether the deceased would miss out on the triumphant return of Christ.

St. Paul responded in the first letter to the Thessalonians (4:13-18) by assuring them that all the faithful will be reunited with the Lord. Then he adapted his understanding of this belief by asserting that when Christ returns, those who have died will be raised up first, then those who are still living will be joined with them, and finally all the faithful will be united with the Lord forever. Paul did not abandon his belief in the second coming of Christ or his conviction that all the faithful would be united with him, but he modified his understanding of that belief to account for the facts of the situation and to alleviate the concerns of his inquirers. He made faith-sense of the Thessalonians' experience by adapting what he already believed.

A modern example of this same process is the Christian response to evolutionary theory and scientific discoveries about the physical makeup and functioning of the world. At first it seemed that evolution contradicted the biblical account of God creating the world in seven days. As the facts supporting evolutionary theory grew, however, Christians modified their understanding of how God created the universe. Some compared the biblical seven days with seven epochs of evolutionary development; others acknowledged that the biblical account is a literary device and the facts about God's creation are left for scientists to fill in. Belief in God as creator was not abandoned but the explanation of this belief was modified to correspond to the facts of experience.

In a similar way, a scientific commitment to the facts and laws of nature raised questions about the traditional Christian understanding of miracles and God's power to intervene in the normal course of events. It seemed that God's miraculous interventions actually violated the very order in nature which God had established. In recent decades, scientists have recognized that there is a certain amount of openness (indeterminacy) and even chaos (lack of a prescribed order) within the natural makeup of creation. This has enabled Christians to modify their understanding of miracles and assert that God intervenes where nature offers undetermined possibilities. Rather than contradicting the laws of nature, God's miracles are consistent with them.

Modifying your understanding of the faith is not a compromise or betrayal. It is a living, dynamic engagement of faith and facts. It is a search for a new, more adequate explanation which harmonizes better with your everyday experience. Obviously you cannot be expected to have such a command of the faith tradition that you can formulate new explanations all at once or all by yourself. Modification is a gradual process. It means you must review and examine your own understanding of the faith; you must be open to the opinions and explanations of others; and you must be willing to modify your favorite understanding when a better explanation appears. Even then, you may struggle for a time trying to make faith-sense of challenging experiences.

There are some experiences that do not fit the faith tradition no matter how hard you try to modify your understanding to accommodate them. For example, Jane's lifelong closest friend, Sue, recently had an extra-marital affair through which she became pregnant. She does not want to tell her husband or end their marriage, and neither does she love the father of the child or want to marry him. Weighing all her options and considering her situation, Sue decides to have an abortion and try to go on with her life as if nothing had happened.

Jane wants to make faith-sense of her friend's decision but no matter how she tries, she cannot modify her understanding to fit Sue's decision. She acknowledges that women in this country have a legal right to abortion, but she does not believe they have a moral right. She understands the argument about privacy and a woman's control of her own body and she is sympathetic to the history of sexism which has oppressed women, but she does not believe that conceiving new life is a strictly private matter or that it falls in the same category as other bodily functions of a woman. She knows there are different theories about the origin of human life, but she believes the whole process of conception, gestation, and birthing is the development of a human person. Jane wants to be supportive of Sue but there is no way she can modify her understanding to agree with the decision Sue has made. Faith-sense cannot be made at the expense of the faith.

REARRANGE YOUR PRIORITIES

A second way of adapting your belief to make faith-sense of challenging experiences is to rearrange your priorities. A clear example of this in the New Testament is the encounter of Peter with the Gentile soldier, Cornelius (Acts 10). It is one of several incidents in which the priorities of the Jewish followers of Jesus had to be rearranged for the sake of Gentile disciples. In this instance Peter had a dream in which God commanded him to eat food that was forbidden by Jewish dietary law. As Peter was trying to make faith-sense of this dream, messengers from Cornelius invited Peter to the centurion's house to instruct him and his family in the ways of Jesus. When Peter arrived, he realized that Cornelius and his household already shared the gift of the Holy Spirit although they had not yet been baptized. Rather than deny his experience, Peter rearranged his priorities (and interpreted his dream), declaring that whoever and whatever is acceptable to God takes precedence over everything else—even the precepts of the Mosaic Law.

A modern example of rearranging priorities is the movement for Christian unity. Historically the mainline churches and denominations have tended to define themselves in opposition to one another while claiming to be a more faithful embodiment of the Church Jesus intended. Denominational identity and self-preservation have been a higher priority than Christian unity. However, the experience of the great missionary effort of the nineteenth century convinced Church leaders that if they were to spread the gospel effectively, they had to overcome their divisions and form a united Church. The effort to do this has occupied the entire twentieth century. It has made ecumenism a higher priority than ever before and given greater importance to ecumenically sensitive rather than antagonistic language, to common projects rather than separate activities, and to formal church unions rather than denominational distinctions.

Rearranging priorities is always a possibility because Christianity is a comprehensive and flexible way of life; it admits many different configurations. The first two commandments, love of

God and love of neighbor, have an irreplaceable priority, but everything else can be ranked differently depending on your circumstances and experiences. When you rearrange your priorities, you are not rejecting the truths and practices of your faith. You are shifting emphasis in order to respond more realistically and effectively to what is happening in your life.

At the same time, rearranging priorities is not like moving chess pieces on a board. Most people feel strongly about their priorities and do not change them easily. When they do, they face a lot of uncertainty and need support and reinforcement to make the transition. For example, Chris has been a mail carrier in a rural community in West Virginia for fifteen years. His personal motto, which he has used to make faith-sense of his work, is the verse from St. Paul (Rom 10:15, which Paul took from Isa 52:7): "How beautiful are the feet of those who bring good news." Of course, he readily admits that he also brings people bills and occasional bad news, but he values his job as a messenger and he also likes to be outdoors "in God's backyard," as he frequently says. It would take a major event for Chris to rearrange his priorities.

In due course that major event took place. Chris began to experience more and more arthritic pain. It finally reached the point where he simply could no longer deliver mail. Faced with a change he had always resisted, he was apprehensive and even thought of retiring. After talking with a number of the people on his mail route, however, he sensed that he could make his new situation meaningful if he rearranged his priorities. Instead of placing primary importance on being a messenger of good news to friends on his route, he began to emphasize his role as a servant of good cheer to strangers who walked into the post office. Instead of finding God in the beauty of nature outdoors, he put more value on seeing old friends when they came to town. In neither case did Chris reject what he previously believed; he simply gave other beliefs priority so he could make faith-sense of his new experience.

ADD TO YOUR PERSPECTIVES

A third way to adapt your beliefs in order to make faith-sense of your experience is to add different perspectives to your usual point of view. This is similar to rearranging priorities, but it is more extensive and more original. It calls for the addition and combining of several beliefs rather than repositioning them in a new order of importance.

A good example of this in the New Testament is the struggle of Jesus' disciples to make faith-sense of his death. It was troubling enough for them that he died at all. However, if they were to convince others that he was the Messiah, they had major problems. He did not fit the traditional image of a powerful, triumphant warrior-king and he avoided all attempts to cast him that way. What was worse, there was no clear expectation that the Messiah should die, and certainly not as a political criminal and a religious blasphemer.

Beginning in chapter two of the Acts of the Apostles, Peter expresses the faith-sense of Jesus' followers by drawing together the following themes: God's plan and foreknowledge (2:23), God's power to overcome Jesus' death through the resurrection rather than prevent it (2:24), the ignorance of the Jews in handing Jesus over to the Romans (3:17), the disciples' own eyewitness experience (4:20), and the mysterious power of suffering (5:41) which St. Paul would extol in his own attempts to make faith-sense of Jesus' death in 1 Cor 1:18-25. No single belief could adequately make faith-sense of Jesus' death but the combination of several beliefs did.

A modern example of this way of making faith-sense is the response of Christians to homosexuality. Although some believers absolutely condemn homosexuality in all respects, most Christians find it a challenge to their faith. The complexity of the issue calls for a response that combines several faith perspectives rather than relying on a single, simple position. The biblical and historical prohibitions of homosexuality are the norm of faith, but they must be interpreted in light of the medical and psychological data available today which were unknown in the past. The addition of this data helps to clarify what the Bible condemns and what it does not condemn.

Likewise, an objective condition of homosexuality may be considered morally "disordered" but that does not negate the moral values of love, fidelity, service, and care which may exist in a same-sex relationship. A homosexual orientation is not all that defines a person as a person, any more than a heterosexual orientation is all there is to say about a person. Doctrinally every person is a human being, made in the image of God with dignity and rights who deserves respect, support, and acceptance. Bringing all these perspectives together is not easy and may not yield a perfectly satisfactory response to the experience of homosexuality, but it is a viable way of making faith-sense of such a complex issue.

Adding different faith perspectives requires a comprehensive outlook rather than a simple, unquestioned position. It is not, however, a speculative or hypothetical exercise in which you try to see how many different beliefs you can think of. Making faith-sense by adding different perspectives is not a quantitative but a qualitative activity. It is a matter of recognizing and bringing together relevant points of view which are suggested by the particular experience you are trying to make sense of.

For example, Ed and Helen are devout Christians, dutiful parents, and concerned citizens. They give top priority to their spiritual life and deal with troubling or challenging situations by turning them over to the Lord in prayer. In this way they make the most important and, in their view, the most effective contribution they can.

One Sunday their pastor informed the congregation that the owner of several adult nightclubs intended to open a new club in their community. Ed and Helen were disturbed by this news but they were even more struck when their pastor said that prayer alone would not prevent the club from opening. He urged everyone to take appropriate action. Ed and Helen wrestled with their pastor's message and their own desire to prevent the bad influence which this club would have. They decided to add action to their prayers.

Over the next several weeks they worked with other members of the congregation and with concerned believers from the denominations in the area; they attended public hearings, wrote letters to the editor of the local newspaper, spoke with city council members, met with the club owner to try to change his mind, and prayed. In trying to make faith-sense of the situation they added to their prayer the faith perspectives of ecumenism, citizenship, advocacy, and persuasiveness.

BENEFITS

When challenged to make faith-sense by adapting your beliefs, you still affirm your faith but you do it differently. You introduce changes that were not there before and you give your faith a new shape in dialogue with your own experience. This has several benefits. First of all, it enlivens your faith and makes it more engaging because your belief is not confined to the formulations and emphases handed on to you. It becomes more dynamic, more real when you adapt it to the concrete situations you face.

Second, your faith also becomes more your own. You have to think it through for yourself rather than rely on someone else to do it for you or repeat what someone else has formulated in their circumstances. This does not mean you do not seek input from others or test your adaptations against their knowledge; it means that you appropriate (literally, make your own) everything available to you in order to make sense of your own experience.

Third, adapting your faith to challenging situations verifies that your belief is not a static, idealistic outlook suitable only for pleasant, positive experiences but not worth much against the troubling, realistic events that occur in everyone's life. People who are willing to modify their explanations, rearrange their priorities, and add to their perspectives are ready to face whatever life hands them and make faith-sense of it.

Of course, these benefits presuppose that your adaptations are consistent with the truth and meaning of the faith. It is always possible to compromise your beliefs or rationalize your adaptations, and this is the biggest concern with this way of making faith-sense. As some of the examples in this section (and throughout the book) point out, not every experience can be harmonized with Christian belief. You must always be vigilant that your attempts to make your faith sensible preserve your faith.

CAUTION

On the other hand, it is possible that you can hold back from making appropriate adaptations because you are not sure of yourself, you are afraid of making a mistake, you cannot foresee the outcome of your actions, or you feel alone in making changes. These are all reactions to be expected and respected, but they should not prevent you from making the adaptations your experience calls for. Partners can be a great aid in overcoming these inhibitions, and in checking any tendencies to compromise or rationalize. But in the final analysis, only you can make faith-sense of your life and sometimes you can do this only by modifying your explanations, rearranging your priorities, or adding new perspectives to what you already believe and what the rest of your experience tends to affirm and illustrate.

EXAMPLE

To concretize further how experience can challenge you to adapt your faith, consider the following example.

Fran was attracted to nursing from the time she volunteered as a teenager to help out at the local hospital. After high school she completed two years of junior college, finished her nursing degree, and, while working full time as a hospital nurse, completed her BS degree as well.

During all this time, Fran has seen her nursing career as a concrete illustration of her faith. The gospel stories of Jesus' healings have been a constant inspiration for her in her contact with patients, and the long-standing tradition of hospitals and healthcare services sponsored by Christian churches has been a great support as she goes about her work. She describes her role as continuing the healing ministry of Jesus and restoring people to as normal a life as their health permits.

Recently Fran's mentor from nursing school called and told her of an opening as administrator of the intensive care unit at a local medical center. She encouraged Fran to apply for it. Fran was hesitant. She did not have a lot of experience with intensive care and it was a management position, which she had not held before. On the other hand, the medical center was a joint Catholic-Methodist venture, formed three years ago when the separate hospitals were struggling to survive. Fran had not been able to work in a religious health care facility and she was attracted to that possibility.

With the urging of her mentor and the support of her husband and friends, Fran applied. After a battery of interviews and committee evaluations, she was hired—to her surprise, and anxiety. However, the transition went smoothly and Fran felt a great deal of support from the nurses and administrators as she learned her new responsibilities. After three months in the job, she realized that this is a different situation which is posing challenges to her not only as a professional but also as a Christian.

The two biggest changes, and challenges, are that over half of her patients die without leaving the ICU and she is now part of management rather than staff or front line workers. These changes mean that her work no longer simply affirms or illustrates her beliefs. To make faith-sense of her current experience, Fran must do more than recall Jesus' healings or the health care commitment of the Christian tradition—valuable as these are.

In conversations with her husband, the hospital chaplain, her mentor, and in private, prayerful reflection, Fran has begun to adapt her beliefs to make faith-sense of her new experience. The first challenge was to deal with the high mortality rate among the ICU patients. To handle this, Fran modified her previous understanding of her work. Instead of describing it as healing and restoring people to their normal life, she began to think of it as helping them to die and preparing them for the new life to follow. Her explanation was still life oriented and grounded in the example of Jesus but now it was modified to fit her current experience.

A more difficult challenge was the management position she now held. Instead of being concerned only for the patients in her immediate care, she had to take into account the whole ICU as well as the other departments of the medical center. This caused her to rearrange her priorities. In addition to the welfare of each patient, she had to consider the best use of the available resources for all the patients in the ICU and at the medical center. Technically this is called triage; theologically, as the pastoral care chaplain informed her, it is called the common good. This doctrinal theme of the Christian tradition has become more important to Fran the longer she works as administrator of the ICU.

Fran had always thought of herself as a nurse and her work as health care, but in her new position she has had to add a few other perspectives. Many of the people in the ICU are there because of poor health conditions in their homes, communities, and social networks. Fran began to realize, as she never had before, that the health of each individual is a reflection of the health of their social environment. This not only gave her a broader perspective on her patients; it also helped her interpret the healings of Jesus. She began to recognize that many of his healings were aimed at social attitudes and practices as well as physical deficiencies (e.g., the man with the withered hand, Matt 12:9-14; the paralytic lowered into the room where Jesus was teaching, Mark 2:1-12; the epileptic man at Gerasene, Luke 8:26-39; the blind man from birth, John 9:1-39).

In addition, as an administrator, she had to reckon with the influence of insurance companies and the possibility of lawsuits. She knew that most of the cost of treating ICU patients came from their insurance carriers. She also knew that if the health care they received was not adequate, the medical center could be sued. She did not want either of these factors to dictate her health care decisions or compromise the faith meaning of her work, but she had to take them into account. In essence, she realized that to make faith-sense of her current experience she had to include more than her faith perspective. She thought of Jesus maintaining his integrity before Pilate (John 18:33-38), and of Christians throughout the ages struggling to live faithfully in hostile societies. For Fran, being a nurse affirmed her faith; being a hospital administrator challenged it.

EXERCISE

Sometimes events challenge you to make faith-sense by adapting your beliefs. To practice this form of making faith-sense, go back to the experience you have been working with, or select a new one, and ask the following questions:

1. Does this experience challenge me to rethink my beliefs and practices in any way? Do I find myself saying "yes, but" in response to an experience, and asking "why?"
2. Does this experience seem to call for a modification of my previous understanding, a rearrangement of my current priorities, an addition to my typical perspectives? If so, which sources of the faith do I use to make these changes?
3. As I make adaptations in my belief, do I find myself a more engaged believer? Does my faith seem more my own? Am I able to face tough, troubling experiences?
4. Am I aware of the risks involved in adapting my faith (compromising, rationalizing, holding back)? Do I have any partners or other resources that can help me recognize and prevent those risks?

Conversion

Occasionally you may have an experience which neither affirms what you already believe nor challenges you to adapt it, but seems to call for a really new understanding or practice of your faith. Such experiences do not happen very often but when they do, they can have a powerful, defining effect which may last a long time. For example, Fran's experience with dying patients or with administering the ICU could lead her beyond adapting her faith to a new understanding of life and death or a new insight into the spiritual meaning of management that could influence her professional future.

When experiences have this kind of impact, they do not challenge you to simply rethink your previous understanding and practice (as in the previous section); they actually challenge you to replace it with a new understanding and practice. The replacement they call for is not outside of or opposed to the faith tradition, i.e., you are not expected to abandon your Christian convictions. Rather you are challenged to take a really new faith position, new at least for you.

The emphasis in experiences like this is not "yes, but" as in the previous section, but more like "whereas, now." The clearest example of this in the New Testament is the Sermon on the

Mount. The formula Jesus uses there (Matt 5:21-48) is: "You have heard it said . . . but I say to you." He was citing experiences and reactions familiar to his listeners (anger, adultery, divorce, oaths, retaliation, hatred) and using them to propose a new way of thinking and acting (reconciliation, sexual fidelity, marital permanence, truthfulness, non-violence, love of enemies). To switch from the familiar, well-established approach to what Jesus advocated was more than an adaptation; it was an innovation. In Christian history it has been called conversion.

Conversion is often thought of as a sudden, dramatic reversal of a person's way of life. The description of St. Paul being knocked down on the road to Damascus is the standard model (Acts 9:3-4). In fact, conversion usually occurs much less flamboyantly and takes a longer period of time. The experience that provokes it may be sudden and dramatic but the actual change to a new way of thinking and acting is usually slower and more mundane.

For example, Betty was raised to believe that the greatest honor for a woman is to be a caring, giving mother. She is married to a loving husband and has three children to whom she has devoted herself completely. Now that they are in high school, she is busier than ever, attending their activities, volunteering at their school, and doing everything she can to meet their needs and help their development. A few months ago she began to experience dizzy spells. When she went to the doctor for a checkup, she learned that she was borderline anemic with high blood pressure and a dangerous cholesterol level. The message from her doctor was succinct: "You better start taking care of yourself or there won't be a self to take care of."

The news stunned Betty. She had dedicated her life to her children, never thinking of her own needs. "I'll have plenty of time for that once they're on their own," she typically said when her husband would ask her to slow down or encourage her to do something for herself. The truth is, she felt that satisfying her own needs and desires was selfish. The needs of her family, as she perceived them, always took precedence. Now she is trying to replace her previous outlook with the view that taking care of herself enables her to care for her family the way she wants to, and they desire. Her new approach is summed up in a phrase she repeats each morning: "Christianity demands self-sacrifice, not self-destruction." Betty meditates on the meaning of that distinction and is trying to put it into practice, with the help of her husband and children who point out when they think she is slipping back into her old ways.

In short, Betty is undergoing a conversion. She is trying to see her life in a new way and to replace one set of convictions with another. In doing so, she remains very much within the Christian context. The lifestyle she is trying to convert to is already practiced by many faithful, loving mothers and is solidly supported by the pastoral care tradition of the Church, but it is genuinely new for Betty. She is learning a lot from those women who share their experience with her verbally and through publications. She is also finding it easier to articulate the changes she wants to make and the values they represent than it is to put them into practice. A change of thinking does not automatically lead to a change of behavior, as will be discussed in the next chapter.

Experiences that seem to call for conversion should be handled like any other experience you want to make faith-sense of. Narrate the experience as factually as possible using the information questions, and analyze its underlying causes. The impetus for conversion may come from either source. At each point of the narration and analysis, pay attention to whether the experience takes the whereas/now form.

For example, the blunt message from her doctor (who) confronted Betty with the need for a substantial change. Whereas she assumed she could keep going as she always had, now she realizes that she must pay more attention to her own physical well being. The risks to her health (what) forced Betty to reexamine her lifestyle and her way of serving her family. Whereas she thought it selfish to look after herself, now she sees it as integral to the service she wants to offer. Betty is at a vulnerable time (when) in her life. Whereas she should expect to enjoy many more years of life with her family, and their families, now she knows she must make changes to ensure that this will happen. With the help and support of family and friends (how), Betty is slowly changing her attitude and behavior. Whereas she tended in the past to do whatever she chose to do, now she listens to the feedback and suggestions of others as part of her decision making.

In analyzing why she has developed health problems, Betty can see that they resulted from a well-intentioned but one-sided and ultimately erroneous way of thinking. Whereas she adopted without question what was expected of wives and mothers in her cultural upbringing, now she is reexamining her assumptions in order to fulfill her role more appropriately.

When your experience prompts this kind of whereas/now evaluation, it will likely touch on one of three areas in your life: your ideas, your values, or your behavior.

IDEAS, VALUES, BEHAVIORS

Ken was raised to believe that God has a single, detailed plan for each person's life. The task of a believing person is to discern God's plan and fulfill it. Ken admits that this belief caused him some anxiety when he chose his career (was this what God wanted him to do?) and even when he decided to marry Susan (was she the one God intended him to marry?), but he always lived by his conviction, praying over every decision until he felt confident he had grasped what God wanted.

Over the past few years, as Ken and Susan's children have been preparing for college, they have reviewed their career options and corresponding programs of study. Melanie wants to work with people but is undecided between physical therapy and social work. Ben is drawn to music and is considering music education, the performing arts, or perhaps the business end of the entertainment industry. The options his children have and their freedom, even excitement, in considering them have challenged Ken's outlook. He hears himself say that he only wants them to be happy and fulfilled; whichever career path helps them to achieve that is fine with him.

This experience has made him wonder whether God feels the same way. Maybe God does not have a detailed plan which each person is expected to conform to; maybe God, like Ken, has broad expectations and works with each person as they make life decisions to help them achieve the fullest measure of happiness they can. Thinking this way has given Ken a new insight into the biblical and doctrinal meaning of the Fatherhood of God and has offered him a new awareness of himself as a sincere and faithful son of that God. In short, Ken is experiencing a conversion in his way of thinking, prompted by his children's development. Whereas he used to think God had a detailed plan for each person's life, now he thinks God has a parent's desire for each person's happiness, and a parent's fidelity in accompanying them in their pursuit of it.

Renee began working in her family's discount clothing business when she was a teenager. After completing college and her MBA degree, she took a more active role in the business, eventually becoming president when her father retired. Since then, she has continued to update the product line, modernize the marketing and advertising strategies, and expand the number of stores. The family business has never been more successful and Renee has taken great satisfaction in contributing to it.

She values her success as a confirmation of the slogan her father used when he started the business: "An honest profit is God's delight—and your reward." This sentiment expresses a long-standing religious conviction that God's favor is manifested in the blessings of a good life. Biblically these include longevity, a large family, and material prosperity. Historically many Christians have looked for similar, tangible signs of God's favor, and money in the bank is about as tangible as a sign can be. Recently these values have been put to the test.

Renee received a buyout offer from a national company which is putting together a large merger. The buyout would make Renee and her whole family independently wealthy for the rest of their lives. It seemed like the ultimate reward from God, except that the buyout would also mean the loss of jobs for some of the long-time employees, the closing of several stores in areas where people had no convenient alternative, and an increase in prices which would be burdensome for many loyal customers whom Renee knows personally.

As she wrestled with her decision, Renee faced a conversion moment. Does she value personal financial gain over the people she has known and served, and who have helped make her successful? If people are made to suffer, is the financial profit honest, and can it be interpreted as a reward from God? Her questions took her back to the Bible and especially to the prophets whose call for justice, care for the poor, and walking rightly with God are preeminent. Renee also consulted with her minister about the Church's moral tradition and how a situation like this might be evaluated. And she could not get one phrase out of her head: "What does it profit someone to gain the whole world yet lose their soul?" (based on Luke 9:25). Renee did not think her salvation was in jeopardy, but her values were.

Renee decided to decline the offer, and in doing so she replaced one value with another. Whereas Renee had believed that an honest profit is a sign of God's favor, and the bigger the profit, the greater God's favor, she now believes that God's favor has little to do with financial wealth—at least, it is not a sure sign of God's blessing. Rather, God's favor rests on those who make morally right decisions for the welfare of other people. This is different from formulating a new understanding of profit or rearranging priorities, both of which could have allowed Renee to accept the buyout offer. She converted from the value of making the most profit (even honestly) to the value of making the best decision, and in the process she made faith-sense of her experience in a new way (for her).

Tyrone was released from prison six weeks ago after serving a five-year term. While in prison, he was greatly influenced by the prison chaplain who helped him turn his life over to Jesus. When he left prison, Tyrone was determined to begin a new life and was confident that with the Lord's help he would succeed. He kept hearing the prison chaplain say, "God will provide," and Tyrone believed it.

However, without a high school diploma and with virtually no work experience, he found it very difficult to get a good job. Even worse, Tyrone was extremely self-conscious about his prison record and did not present himself very well in interviews, having learned to be docile and non-assertive in the prison environment. When none of his initial interviews led to a job, he began to tell himself that no one would hire him because he was an ex-felon.

For a few weeks now Tyrone has been feeling very sorry for himself. He sneers sarcastically when the phrase, "God will provide," comes to mind. He spends most of the day watching television while his mother and brother, with whom he lives, are working. He does not want to take advantage of them but he feels discouraged and does not know what to do. He has all but given up the effort to start over.

One day he went out for a pack of cigarettes and while sitting in traffic, he noticed a bumper sticker on the car in front of him. It read: "The best way to get back on your feet is to get off your butt." Tyrone laughed out loud. The saying, which he assumed was intended for people on welfare, fit him perfectly. It challenged the defeatist attitude he had been adopting and made him take a fresh look at himself. He did not want to be the person he was becoming. On his way home another saying popped into his mind, one which his mother used a lot. "God helps those who help themselves." Tyrone was at a point of conversion, prompted by a commonplace part of popular culture—a bumper sticker.

Over the next several days he gradually replaced one set of behaviors with another. Instead of sitting around waiting for God (or someone) to change his life for him, Tyrone decided to spend each day looking for work. He left the house in the morning with his mother and brother and did not return until they did. During the day, he went to as many interviews and made as many job applications as he could. He practiced presenting himself to would-be employers and describing his positive qualities. He compiled all the work assignments he had had in prison and even listed one of the prison guards who supervised his work detail as a reference. Eventually, Tyrone was hired as a maintenance worker at the local junior college.

Tyrone's conversion is not yet complete and he knows it, but he also knows he has made the right changes. He has not abandoned the faith which he discovered in prison, but he has replaced one way of carrying it out with another. Whereas he had expected Jesus to come in and make everything right in his life, now he feels he is literally handing his life over to Jesus by the actions he is taking.

ASSUMPTIONS

Experiences which stimulate a conversion in your thinking, your values, or your behavior all have one thing in common: they expose and question what you have assumed or taken for granted. Betty assumed she would always be able to give to her family without regarding what it took out of her; Renee assumed that financial profit was a sure sign of God's favor as long as it was honestly acquired; Tyrone took for granted that he could turn his life around because God would provide.

Experiences that call for conversion expose the limitations and inadequacies of your assumptions. This does not mean you are at fault for holding these assumptions or that they are completely wrong; it means that your experience up to this point has not conflicted with what you have taken for granted. There has been no need to question, or even be aware of, your assumptions. However, when new or different experiences occur, they can challenge you to reconsider the adequacy of what you had taken for granted. The intent is not to make life more complicated but to make your faith more livable. A modern example of this is ecology.

For centuries Christians took nature for granted. The Bible proclaimed it as a gift from God, over which humankind was given dominion (Gen 1:26). The historical shift from agriculture to industry was interpreted, doctrinally, as a progression toward greater mastery of nature, improvement of life, and glory for God. The moral issues raised in connection with this development were exclusively human concerns: the exploitation of workers, the disruption of traditional family and cultural life, the creation of separate and antagonistic economic classes, the disproportionate use of the earth's resources by a small percentage of the earth's population.

These were (and are) real moral problems, but they neglect the equally moral claims of creation itself on human beings: the destruction of delicate ecosystems, the upsetting of natural habitats, the endangering of plant and animal species, the loss of irreplaceable resources. The moral claims of creation were muted somewhat by the aesthetic, and at times romantic, use of nature in public worship, but this did not lead Christians to see the environment as having intrinsic value, apart from its value to human beings.

When scientists began to chart the devastation to creation through pollution, waste, neglect, and lack of planning, they also confronted Christians with their assumptions and what they had taken for granted. The prospect that the earth might no longer sustain life, including human life, shattered the easy conviction that God would see to it that we survive. Human responsibility figured more prominently into the equation and human behavior had to change for the sake of life itself. The ecological experience called for a global conversion in thinking, values, and action.

Christians have responded in various ways. Some have cited the ecological crisis as a reminder of God's judgment against human pride and greed, and an illustration of the destruction of the world to come. Others have adapted their beliefs, modifying the understanding of Genesis by re-defining dominion as stewardship, rearranging priorities so that human desires and ambitions are not automatically given first place, and adding different perspectives such as eco-spirituality, environmental morality, and redemption of the world—not just of humans.

Those who see the ecological crisis as a conversion experience are moved to go further as their assumptions are critiqued. Whereas most Christians, relying on the traditional interpretation of Genesis, think of the world as created for the sake of human beings, ecologically converted Christians prefer to think of the world as created with us, or even as our being created for the sake of the world, as its servant, in the spirit of the incarnation whereby God became not merely human, but the servant of all (Phil 2:5-8). In this spirit they replace even the idea of stewardship with the idea of partnership and assert that creation itself has rights and claims which are at least coequal with those of human beings. Some push this point to the extreme of saying that "animals are people too," but the notion that animals and other living things have rights is an innovative way of thinking about ecology within the Christian tradition.

Christians who have experienced an ecological conversion replace the value of developing creation with the value of reverencing it. Whereas they used to appreciate creation as a treasury of natural resources to be harnessed and adapted to enhance human life, now they relate to creation as a living source of experience and meaning. While natural resources are still used to enhance human life, the enhancement is not measured simply in terms of the material well-being of humans (and not all humans at that). Respect for living things and a mutual relationship with nature have led many to a new kind of spiritual ecumenism with native Americans, eastern mystics, and other traditions having a holistic view of life.

Finally, ecologically converted Christians are challenged to translate their ideas and values into behaviors. Whereas they assumed the natural environment was a given, available for the support and advancement of human life, they now realize they have a responsibility to care for it, protect it, cultivate it, and actively defend it. In doing so, they are replacing learned habits that were taken for granted with specific practices consciously chosen. These range from vegetarian eating patterns to a simple lifestyle, avoiding disposable products and recycling waste, beautifying environments and preventing litter, protecting wildlands and securing animal sanctuaries, establishing environmental controls and penalizing those who violate them. Many of these actions have become part of the daily lifestyle and conscious behavior of committed Christians, adding ecology to the way of life which characterizes a follower of Jesus.

Experiences that prompt a conversion in your ideas, values, and behavior are usually not isolated, passing events. They are deep-rooted, substantial occurrences that affect your life, or the life of your community, as a whole: the development of nuclear energy, the civil rights movement, the Vietnam War, the Second Vatican Council, the contraceptive pill, the exploration of space, the collapse of the Soviet Union, the rise of feminism, the emergence of the personal computer, the threat to the environment, the formation of a global economy. These are typically the events that call into question what you have taken for granted and cause you to re-examine and perhaps replace what you have thought, what you have valued, and what you have done.

Conversion experiences of this type do not occur very often and when they do, they tend to impact individuals as members of a group or part of a generation rather than strictly as individuals. Betty, Ken, Renee, and Tyrone in the examples above are representative of their generation, culture, and social class as much as they are unique individuals. For this reason, when events suggest a conversion of ideas, values, or behaviors in order to make faith-sense of your experience, it is a good bet that other believers with your background and in your circumstances are being challenged to do the same.

This is a forceful reminder that your faith is not divorced from the rest of your life. What happens in history and society, in medicine and technology, in culture and science, in fashion and business, in politics and entertainment affects what you take for granted and what you submit to scrutiny, what you presuppose and what you need to have proven. This same attitude carries over to your faith life and affects what you believe, how you believe, and what sort of faith-sense you make of the world in which you live.

BENEFITS

As with affirmation and adaptation, making faith-sense through conversion reinforces and makes relevant what you believe in relation to what you experience in your everyday life. But conversion has additional benefits. It fosters creativity to a greater degree than either affirmation or adaptation. When really new experiences challenge your faith, they call for really new responses. This in turn requires a greater degree of creativity as you search for alternatives, explore new possibilities, and put together a fresh way of thinking, valuing, and acting. A creative faith is a living faith and much more likely to enhance your experience than a routine, familiar, and unchanging system of beliefs.

At the same time, creativity cultivates a spirit of freedom with regard to your faith. This does not mean that "anything goes" or that you can make the faith be anything you want. It means that you do not feel rigidly bound to the formulas and practices you inherited and learned, much less that you feel afraid to question or change them. This kind of freedom characterized Jesus' manner of seeing things, of responding to people, and of making his own decisions. As St. Paul declared to the Galatians (5:1): "For freedom Christ set us free." Making innovative faith-sense perpetuates this central Christian value.

Finally, the experience of conversion and the creative freedom to make innovations put you in the mainstream of Christianity's dynamic power. This is the richest meaning of tradition, which is a hallmark of Christian faith. But tradition does not mean a static collection of teachings and practices preserved intact. It means a living community of people claiming their heritage by the creative way they continue to live it in changing situations. Making faith-sense through conversion confirms your status as a member of a dynamic tradition and enables you to offer your own special contribution to that ongoing process. On the other hand, you should not be too quick to dismiss what has been developed and established by your predecessors in the faith or to assume that it does not make sense simply because it does not make sense to you. With the creative freedom of innovation comes a heightened responsibility to know the tradition, value its accomplishments, and test your own impulses before actually making changes.

CAUTION

The greatest caution in this regard is that you maintain an attitude of respect and care when you feel challenged by your experience to convert your thinking, values, or behaviors. Reckless replacements and self-righteous innovations are not consistent with the meaning of faith-sense and do not promote the goal of dynamic Christian living. A conversion experience can be an exciting, fulfilling moment but it should always remain a conversion of faith.

EXAMPLE

George is a junior in college. He comes from a middle class background and was raised with strong Christian beliefs and values. At college he has met many classmates with different orientations, but he has not felt challenged to reexamine his own beliefs or behaviors. If anything, he is more convinced than ever of his Christian way of life—and grateful for it.

One of his college courses is a survey of modern social changes. He was already familiar with the civil rights movement and sympathetic to its goals and accomplishments. He was also well aware of the ecological movement and has been supportive of it in his own lifestyle. The discussion of feminism, however, has been a real eye-opener for him. George was raised to respect women, and he deeply values their unique role as mothers. He believes firmly in equal rights for women and supports equal opportunity policies.

Until this course, however, George did not realize how much of his culture (and church) is dominated by a one-sided, male point of view. Through assigned readings, the professor's lectures, and discussions with his classmates, he has begun to recognize how a male perspective is simply taken for granted as superior and normative. Rational thinking (associated with men) is preferred to sensitive feeling (associated with women); production and construction (tendencies of men) are valued more than sharing and relating (tendencies of women); leadership is defined as asserting direction (a male style) rather than eliciting consensus (a female style); individual accomplishment (a male goal) is prized over communal advancement (a female goal).

As his consciousness is raised, George's assumptions are exposed. He feels challenged to make even more basic changes in his thinking, values, and behavior, which he felt were already quite liberated. He is grappling with a conversion experience that requires innovations if he is to make faith-sense of it.

For example, George's idea of God has been implicitly male. This is partly the result of depictions in religious art; largely it is the result of language. In George's experience God has always been referred to as "he." While George realizes that God is beyond gender, the constant masculine references subtly promote the assumption that God really is masculine, or at least more masculine than feminine. This further presupposes (without being stated explicitly) that typical male ways of thinking and acting must be closer to God's ways and therefore normative for both men and women.

Whereas George took masculine references to God for granted, now he has begun to use female references for God in his private prayer and reflection. In conversations and occasional writing, he tries to find alternative constructions which are neither male nor female. At the very least, he is training himself to be sensitive to the exclusive use of male references and when appropriate, to recommend other ways of speaking. It is a slow, awkward, and frustrating process, but George knows he is making better faith-sense now than he did before he took the course because he is replacing a one-sided, inadequate idea of God with a fuller, more accurate concept.

Similarly, George never paid too much attention to how Jesus treated women. He always assumed that the main point of the gospel stories was a general message of Jesus' encounters with women. Now as he re-reads those incidents, with the help of women commentators, he realizes how innovative and free Jesus actually was. Whenever Jesus met women who embodied the reign of God which he proclaimed, he drew attention to them and held them up as models for both men and women to imitate.

Whereas George has valued women as equal to men and complementary to men's qualities and capacities, now he is learning to value women in their own right as whole persons with inherently valuable qualities and capacities of their own. He tries not to speak of women as equal to men because that presupposes that men are still the standard; he tries to avoid the word complementary because that defines women from a male perspective instead of a female perspective. Most of all, he tries to value women for who they say they are and how they express their own intrinsic worth. It is clumsy at times but also humorous, rewarding, and stimulating for George's awareness of himself as a man.

Finally, in his review of Jesus' experience with women George was struck by the occasions when a woman seemed to change Jesus' mind or influence his action. He thought of the Syro-Phoenician woman asking help for her child (Mark 7:25-30), of Jesus' mother at the wedding celebration in Cana (John 2:1-10), of Mary at the tomb of Lazarus (John 11:28-44). These incidents made George re-evaluate his own reactions to the suggestions of women.

Whereas he had always tried to act in the best interests of women as he defined them, now George determined to suspend his own (presumably superior) sense of things and act on the recommendations of women. A simple opportunity arose when Heather, a friend, suggested what he might give his mother for her birthday. It was not what he had been thinking of, so his first impulse was to politely dismiss her idea. Then he reconsidered and acted on her suggestion. His mother said it was the most meaningful gift he had ever given her, and how did he ever think of it? George interpreted her question as rhetorical and did not answer, but later realized that he had taken credit for Heather's suggestion. Recognizing that this was typical of the behavior he was trying to change, he told his mother about Heather's idea and he told Heather about his mother's reaction. George learned that changing behavior is always more difficult than changing ideas or values, even when you are trying to make faith-sense.

EXERCISE

Occasionally an experience is so substantial and so powerful that it challenges you to make faith-sense by introducing real innovations in your beliefs. When you feel moved toward a conversion of this type, ask yourself:

1. Do I find myself saying, "whereas . . . now" in response to this experience?
2. Does this experience call for innovations in my customary way of thinking, valuing, and acting? Is my experience part of a larger trend or movement in society and the Church?
3. Does this experience expose my assumptions and other factors I have taken for granted? If so, what are they?
4. If I feel moved to make real changes, do I also feel a sense of creativity, freedom, and participation in the dynamic quality of faith life? Am I respectful of the tradition and careful as I make innovations?

The heart of making faith-sense is a reflective exercise but it is not complete until the fruit of your reflection is put into practice. What this entails is described and illustrated in the next chapter.

CHAPTER FOUR

Enacting Faith-Sense:
The Culmination of the Process

The final step in the process of making faith-sense is *enactment*. This also corresponds to the last letter, "E," in the shorthand description, NAME. Although it is presented here as a separate chapter, enactment is integral to the whole process. In fact, you have not made faith-sense until you have turned your reflection into action. This is not just a requirement of the method presented in this book; it is an essential part of what it means to be a Christian.

Christianity is first of all a way of life, not a philosophical or theoretical system of ideas. It should make sense intellectually, of course, but the purpose of making faith-sense is to live faith-fully. Nowhere in the New Testament is this connection stated more bluntly or unmistakably than in the letter of James. "Be doers of the word and not hearers only," says the author (1:22), who then paints a graphic description of what this means. "If a brother or sister has nothing to wear and has no food for the day, and one of you says to them, 'Go in peace, keep warm, and eat well,' but you do not give them the necessities of the body, what good is it? So also faith of itself, if it does not have works, is dead" (2:15-17). The enactment phase of making faith-sense is intended to keep your faith alive. However, putting your faith into practice is not as simple as it may sound.

Obstacles to Enactment

First of all, when you begin with an insight or conviction you arrived at through reflection and discussion, you are functioning in a different way from when you take action. Understanding is not acting; ideas are not behaviors. St. Paul recognized this difference in himself and confessed it with characteristic frankness. "What I do, I do not understand. . . . For I do not do the good I want, but I do the evil I do not want" (Rom 7:15, 19).

Betty, in the example from chapter three, struggles with this same difficulty. She knows in her head that she must take better care of her health, but knowing this does not mean she will automatically do it. She has to translate her understanding into concrete, behavioral actions. For example, instead of doing everything she possibly can for her family, she now chooses one activity each day and puts all her energy and enthusiasm into it. Through this deliberate enactment she is demonstrating her love for her family in a way that is consistent with the faith-sense she made of her current health condition.

George, whose situation was also described in chapter three, faces a similar challenge. As he tries to implement his new awareness of women, he is taking specific steps to put this into practice consistently. It is not enough to recognize that the faith tradition has been dominated by men; he is using feminine references in his personal prayer and avoiding male references to God in his language. Even more striking, he is putting into practice the suggestions and recommendations of women when he makes decisions or carries out tasks. It is a slow and sometimes disappointing effort, but without it George's faith-sense remains a conceptual exercise, not a way of life.

A second problem in putting your faith-sense into practice is that you may not feel comfortable with the practical implications of your reflection. Until you experience yourself speaking and acting differently, you do not know what it will feel like or how you will feel about yourself. St. Peter faced this tension in his relations with Gentile converts. At first he mingled and ate with them freely, but when some strict Jewish Christians showed up, he seemed embarrassed and began to withdraw from association with the Gentile Christians. St. Paul, of course, did not let this behavior go unchallenged (Gal 2:11-14), perhaps being a little insensitive to how difficult it was for Peter to feel comfortable doing something he had avoided his entire life.

Fran, in another of the examples from chapter three, experienced a similar discomfort in her transition from hands-on health care to the management of a relatively unfamiliar unit, the ICU. The tendency in a case like this is to preserve as much as possible the former, familiar situation. The problem with this response is that it prevents you from arriving at a new comfort level. You cannot move on by staying put. Only as Fran experiences herself helping to heal people through her administration, and as she feels satisfied with preparing people to die rather than prolonging their lives will she be able to put into practice the faith-sense she discovered in her new position. And until she does, her faith-sense remains an unrealized possibility, and her professional service will be less than she wants it to be.

George undoubtedly is going through the same kind of discomfort as he adapts his language to fit his new insight and learns to take women's opinions more seriously, shaping his own decisions in relation to them. At first all he is aware of is that he is acting differently; eventually he will realize that he is living out consistently the faith-sense he recognized and affirmed intellectually.

A third obstacle to putting your faith-sense into practice is that you may not have the resources or be in a position to implement what you want to do, especially if you have to rely on others who have not been part of your experience and reflection. St. Paul experienced this more than once when he was prevented from visiting his communities because of bad weather, shipwreck, more urgent problems, illness, or imprisonment (2 Cor 1:5-17; Col 4:7-9; 2 Tim 1:4-5). On one occasion he was abandoned by his traveling companion, John-Mark (Acts 13:13), which led to a falling out with his close friend, Barnabas (Acts 15:36-41).

Tyrone, the ex-felon mentioned in chapter three, certainly faced this obstacle. He knew the importance of a job and he wanted to practice the faith-sense he had acquired in prison by working, but he had to rely on someone else to hire him (like the vineyard workers in Jesus' parable, recorded in Matt 20:1-7). This was not all. He had to counteract the societal stigma attached to criminals which required him to put forth more effort than normal in order to reach his goals. When he was in prison contemplating his new life, Tyrone had no idea how difficult it would be just to get started or how much he would depend on others to help him.

Similarly, George is able to modify his own views of women and change his way of speaking (and praying) but he cannot impose this on his friends or prevent their insensitivity and assumption of male superiority. He can do what is possible for him, but it may fall short of what he wants. Not everyone he knows took the course that opened his eyes, and most of his friends are not at the same level he is with regard to women. They may even make fun of his efforts to practice gender inclusive language and let women's viewpoints influence his own. Enacting faith-sense is rarely a one time, once and for all action. And it is not always unopposed.

A fourth difficulty in putting faith-sense into practice is the influence of instincts and habits. Despite his Christian conversion, Tyrone probably felt a lot of anger and resentment each time he was rejected for work. He could easily have acted out his anger and given in to his instinct to retaliate, even though it would have violated his faith-sense in principle. Deep-seated instincts are hard to tame; even Peter was ready to draw the sword to defend the Prince of Peace.

Habits have the same effect. Habits are repeated actions that can make life easier because you do not have to take time to think through what you do. But habits should be reserved for daily, insignificant tasks so you can think through and make decisions about the more important events in your day. George caught himself in this trap when he dismissed Heather's gift suggestion because he assumed, as he always had, that he knew better. Betty had developed such a habitual way of responding to her family's needs that she never examined it until she became ill. Taking time to think things through is what making faith-sense is all about, and this applies to the enactment phase as well as the narrating, analyzing, and meaning phases.

Although enacting faith-sense is not automatic, there is a natural impulse to put new and meaningful insights into practice.

In doing so, your most important concern is that your practice actually flow from the reflection that goes into making faith-sense. Coming up with reasons to do what you would have done without reflection is not making faith-sense; it is rationalizing or justifying a predetermined action. Renee could have done this by accepting the buyout offer, described in chapter three, as another indication that material success is a sign of God's favor. Instead, she reflected on the circumstances of this new situation and let her reflection guide her to an uncharacteristic decision. Her action flowed from her reflection; she did not first decide what to do, then look for ways to explain it.

On the other hand, taking an abstract principle or value and looking for opportunities to implement it is not faith-sense either; it is applied, and sometimes enforced, religion. George could fall into this pattern with his new-found conviction about women. Instead of letting each experience suggest whether and to what extent a new practice is called for, he could, for example, seize upon every situation to insist on gender-inclusive language and to correct those who violate his sense of this principle—perhaps defeating the very purpose of his action by doing so.

The key to keeping your enactment in harmony with your reflection is to honor the starting point of the whole process. Making faith-sense begins with concrete experience; that same experience is the criterion for shaping an appropriate enactment of your reflection. To put it another way, the enactment of faith-sense is the carrying out of the meaning you have drawn from the experience. After you narrate and analyze your experience, you determine whether its meaning is an affirmation, modification, or conversion of your faith. Then you turn around, as it were, and re-enter the experience at the point which appealed to you the most, equipped now with the faith-sense you have discovered.

Your point of re-entry could be the people in the situation (the answer to the "who" question in the narration); it could be the issues or values in the situation (the "what" question in the narration); it could be the circumstances of the situation (the "where, when, and how" of the narration and especially the "why" question of the analysis). Your enactment is your decision about what to do with regard to the people, the issues, or the circumstances of the experience you have made faith-sense of. It is possible, of course, to enact your faith-sense in relation to more than one of these areas; in fact, it is ultimately the desired goal of making faith-sense. However, for purposes of explanation, and perhaps if you are not yet very familiar with this sort of process, a simpler enactment is appropriate.

Planning

Every enactment of your faith-sense can be enhanced with a little planning. The planning need not be elaborate or overly ambitious. It only has to anticipate what will be required to put a course of action into motion. The basic information questions used to narrate your experience can serve as a helpful framework for doing this.

It is usually appropriate to start with the question *what*. What is the action you will implement? For example, Pam wants to become more involved with The Cubicle Crew's fund raisers; Betty is going to concentrate on one act of service for her family per day; Fran wants to hold regular meetings with the nurses in the ICU; Tyrone is going to interview for a job. It helps to describe the action as concretely and behaviorally as possible, as if you could visualize it before it actually takes place.

The next key question is *who*. Who is involved in the action; who is affected by it; who is needed to accomplish it? The Cubicle Crew is involved in Pam's action; the recipients of the fund raiser are affected by it; all the employees are needed to make it work. Spelling out who is part of the action helps to determine how feasible it is. If The Cubicle Crew needed the support of the company's executives or depended on media coverage to achieve their goals, their enactment might not be successful.

The next question is extremely important. *When* will the enactment take place? Depending on the action, this might be a one-time event or a series of activities leading up to the main event. All preliminary steps should be included as part of the planning for the enactment. If Fran wants to hold regular meetings with the nurses to enact the faith-sense of her new position, she has to determine how often they should meet, the most convenient time for everyone to meet, and how much advance notice she should give them. Each of these steps has its own time frame and should be part of Fran's plan.

The question of *where* an enactment takes place can have a lot to do with the success of its outcome. Fran's meetings might be more beneficial if they are held away from the hospital where everyone works. On the other hand, George's desire to foster gender-inclusive language might not be best enacted if he changes on his own a passage from Scripture he reads in the setting of public worship. Unless the people are properly prepared (going back to the first question), they may find his change of words or phrases a distraction, an annoyance, or even an insult to their biblical and liturgical sense. George will have enacted his faith-sense, but where he did it severely limited its effectiveness.

In one sense the *how* question is already partially answered by determining who is involved, and when and where the action will be implemented. However, determining how to implement your faith-sense includes other considerations. The Cubicle Crew must take several factors into account in deciding on the theme, food, and arrangements for the next fund raiser. They must also select the recipients, invite them to the lunch, transport them if necessary, and make them feel welcome.

The more detailed your analysis of how to put your faith-sense into practice, the more likely you are to succeed. Tyrone has to do more than just show up for an interview. He has to know where the work site is, how he is going to get there, and how long it will take him. He has to plan what to wear, how to fill out the application, and how to conduct himself if there is a personal interview. He should also decide whether to follow up the interview with a thank you, and whether to make an inquiry if he does not hear anything after a reasonable time period.

Each of the steps in planning how to enact your faith-sense is part of the enactment. Any one of them taken in isolation may not seem to have much to do with living a Christian faith life, but all of them taken together are the necessary means for putting your faith into practice. There would have been no last supper if Jesus' disciples had not made the preparations as he instructed them (Luke 22:7-13). They probably wondered what the man with the water jar had to do with the Passover meal, but it all led to an enactment that is continued to this day.

Faith-Style

Enacting your faith-sense consistently and carefully contributes to a lifestyle of faith, or faith-style. In our culture lifestyle is often associated with external and superficial aspects of life—status, image, fashion, possessions. In this sense style is often contrasted with substance, implying that a person's lifestyle is designed to create an impression that may be false or misleading. However, lifestyle can also have a more substantive and valuable connotation.

A style is a way of doing things which ultimately expresses who you are. Authors develop a distinctive writing style, speakers have a certain rhetorical style, and business leaders adopt a particular management style. In the same way, a Christian faith-style is a way of doing things that reflects your commitment to Jesus and who you are as his follower. A faith-style that is nurtured by making faith-sense keeps you alert to what is happening in your life, sensitive to the faith meaning of events, practical in shaping future experiences, and confident that God is present in all areas of your life and that spiritual meaning may be found or created there. When this becomes your faith-style, the reflection process has served its purpose, and life makes its greatest sense.

EXAMPLE

To concretize the enactment phase of making faith-sense, consider the main examples that illustrated the three types of faith meaning discussed in chapter three: Pam and The Cubicle Crew (affirmation), Fran and the ICU (adaptation), and a Christian response to the ecological crisis (conversion).

Pam found herself in a typical job until she was introduced to The Cubicle Crew and its fund-raising activities. In one sense this experience was extraneous to the job itself; in another sense it was the work setting which made possible and sustained the charitable efforts of the Crew. Pam was drawn to this experience in two ways. One was the people, both the members of The Cubicle Crew (her co-workers) and also the recipients of their charitable activity. Both reminded her of many biblical and historical parallels. The other entry point was the issue of helping others in a spirit of Christian charity (illustrating her doctrinal and moral faith tradition) which had an unexpected overlap with Pam's experience of worship.

Filled with an awareness of these affirmations, Pam re-entered the experience, seeking to enact her faith-meaning in relation to the people and issues that attracted her. After a few months, she recognized a perfect way to enact what she was experiencing. Pam volunteered to become a member of The Cubicle Crew. This meant that she would help with the planning, advertising, arranging, and cleaning up after each event, but her real reason for volunteering was that it brought her into closer contact with the recipients.

She had been impressed that The Cubicle Crew wanted the recipients to be present at the fund-raising events but did not want to embarrass or exploit them in any way. She wanted to preserve that value while getting to know the recipients better (another "people" value in this experience). The extra work seemed a small price to pay, especially because she experienced a new sense of community with the other members of the Crew in carrying out their responsibilities. Pam's enactment was tied in to her original experience and enabled her to put into practice the faith-sense that experience had offered her—an illustration of Christian charity, respect for the dignity of others, and community in the act of service. She rightly felt that her enactment was placing her in the mainstream of women and men throughout the ages who themselves had enacted the same values and handed on a living illustration of the faith.

Fran's promotion to supervisor of the ICU caused her to focus on the circumstances of her situation which in turn required her to adapt her previous faith-sense of nursing. The two major circumstances were the mortality rate of her ICU patients and the new responsibilities of managing. These twin factors led her to formulate a new understanding of healing, to rearrange her priorities, and to adapt her faith-sense to include societal conditions.

Finding herself in this new position with new experiences, Fran re-entered the situation with her adapted faith-sense. Whereas she had previously concentrated on the healing and well-being of individual patients, now she concentrated on the support and well-being of her nurses. Fran saw her position as an opportunity to nurture the caregivers in her charge. She did this both informally and privately in one-to-one encounters and more formally in group debriefings, case reviews, and end-of-the-month celebrations. In each setting she tried to elicit feedback, listen attentively, and arrive at consensus about what to do in the ICU.

Her actions were consistent with her modified understanding of healing, her new (management) priority regarding the total well-being of everyone in the health care system, and her additional perspective that societal conditions (including the lives of the nurses outside the hospital) were part of the healing ministry. She herself was learning a new style and did not always succeed at it, but she was enacting the faith-sense which her experience and new situation offered her. And in doing so, she began to identify more closely with Jesus when he instructed, supported, shared with, and entrusted his mission to the disciples. She did not pretend to be a messiah but her daily enactment of her faith-sense drew her unexpectedly into a new and deeper relationship with the Messiah.

The ecological crisis has affected Christians in various ways. Those who have been brought to a point of conversion with regard to their attitude and use of natural resources are likely to enter this experience at the level of the why and how questions. In answer to why the planet is polluted and in jeopardy, the fundamental response is that we humans have not respected and reverenced creation as God did in creating it in the first place. In answer to how this attitude may be achieved, ecologically converted Christians engage in an array of activities which go beyond the requirements of environmental laws, the preferences of environmental etiquette, and the idealism of romantic infatuation.

Ecologically converted Christians re-enter the environmental experience keenly attuned to two reference points, reflected in the information questions: where and when? The answers are here and now. What such Christians do to protect and enhance the natural environment is almost less important than acting with urgency in the immediate circumstances of their lives. Every action is a contribution; there is no logical sequence to be followed or set of preliminary steps to be taken before getting to the "real" action. And no time can be wasted.

This attitude is an innovation in the typical response of Christians toward social problems throughout history. The first generations of Christians anticipated the imminent return of Jesus and were not overly concerned about correcting the imperfections of the world around them. Later Christians, except for those who continued to expect God's sudden intervention and judgment, tended to rely on the gradual influence of God's grace to correct wrongs and move history toward its fulfillment. As a result, Christians tolerated slavery, subordinated women, cultivated docility and acquiescence, identified with the sufferings of Jesus, and held on to the promise of reward in the next life. Whether intended or not, this cluster of attitudes has conspired to lighten the sense of human responsibility for solving worldly problems and weaken the urgency for making radical changes.

Ecologically converted Christians introduce two innovations into this tradition. First, they take a new, proactive role in trying to reverse ecological destruction and, second, they make the natural environment an important part of the Christian agenda. Regarding the first point, there is no indication that God will intervene to save us from ourselves. The ecological crisis is the result of human action and its correction must be the result of human action. While not converting to a pelagian, we-can-save-ourselves-by-our-own-works mentality, ecologically converted Christians advocate a more urgent and important role for human action than has traditionally been the case. In the same way they promote the environment as a higher priority in the spiritual, moral, and liturgical practice of the Church than ever before.

Although these are innovations (but not contradictions) in the faith tradition of Christianity, they are perfectly consistent with the circumstances and experience of the environment today. In other words, the ecological crisis, which calls for an innovative type of faith-sense, also calls for the type of enactment which ecologically converted Christians are making. The starting point for making faith-sense is also the criterion for enacting it.

EXERCISE

Enacting your faith-sense completes the process of making faith-sense. To practice your skill in this phase of making faith-sense, go back to the original experience you have been working with, or select a new one, and ask:

1. What obstacles do I face in making this enactment, e.g., a shift from thinking to acting, personal discomfort with what it implies for me, a lack of resources or a dependence on others to make it work, inhibiting instincts or habits?
2. Is this enactment the result of my reflection on the experience or did I have this action in mind from the outset?
3. Have I planned this enactment? What is the action? Who is involved in it, affected by it, needed to carry it out? When and where will I implement it? How will I proceed, what steps do I have to take?
4. Does this enactment contribute to my Christian faith-style? Is enacting my faith-sense moving me toward prayer?

Conclusion

The process of making faith-sense laid out in this book is thorough, demanding, and challenging. It inevitably raises a basic question: is it worth the effort? Obviously I think it is. Here is why.

1. RATIONAL/INTELLECTUAL SATISFACTION

To make faith-sense of your life is the intelligent thing to do; it satisfies the rational dimension of being human. Although the New Testament exhorts Christians not to be deceived by clever arguments or impressed by tricky rhetoric (2 Tim 4:3-4), it also reminds each one to be prepared to give an explanation for the hope that comes from faith (1 Pet 3:15). Faith is not irrational or un-rational or anti-rational; it is supra-rational. It affirms a truth and a meaning that transcend unaided human intelligence. This does not mean we should not try to understand God's mysteries; it means we should keep trying to understand them, as they occur in our daily lives, without pretending to achieve a final or complete grasp of them.

Making faith-sense satisfies the human craving for intelligence and extends the reach of rational thought into the mysteries of God and God's relationship to creation. Since we are part of this relationship and continue to advance it through our own experience, making faith-sense is a rationally satisfying, intellectually important human activity.

2. EMOTIONAL-PSYCHOLOGICAL CONFIDENCE

To make faith-sense provides emotional confidence and psychological affirmation for our decisions and actions. Human beings are characteristically creative; we usually sense a range of options for acting in any situation—unlike animals and other living things which are basically designed to perform a limited set of functions and to perform them in a predictable way. However, human creativity can also cause uncertainty about which options to choose, and even anxiety about making a wrong (or inferior) choice which cannot be undone.

Making faith-sense can provide emotional-psychological confidence because it anchors your experience in a framework of tested understandings and practices which relate directly to your relationship with God. This framework need not be taken as absolute or unquestionable but as the collective wisdom of believers, handed on for the benefit of you and other current believers. It relieves you of the need to construct meaning by yourself, and provides you with a reasonably reliable guide for relating to God.

SOCIAL SOLIDARITY

To make faith-sense of your life strengthens your solidarity as a social being with other people. This reflects the fact that God has revealed to us and saved us as a people, not as isolated individuals. In the same way we make faith-sense together because we are not alone.

In a religious context, and specifically within Christianity, the name given to this social solidarity is tradition. Tradition is best understood as a verb rather than a noun. It is a process of handing on the experiences, values, and principles from one group to the next, usually in historical or generational sequence.

Tradition locates you in a human context of meaning; it reaffirms your experience of belonging and strengthens the social ties which make you human. Tradition also contributes to the other two factors already mentioned: rational satisfaction and emotional confidence. The more you know your faith tradition, understand how people in different circumstances faced similar questions or challenges, grasp how they responded and why, the more intelligent your efforts to make faith-sense will be. In this case tradition offers not only a treasury of information but also a wealth of stimulation to satisfy the craving of human reason.

In the same way tradition provides precedent, the example of real people in real situations grappling with alternatives, making decisions, and leaving behind the testimony of their efforts. This gives you greater confidence in facing present day challenges, weighing options, and anticipating consequences. It is as if you have all the ancestors in faith as your counselors.

Making faith-sense enables you to participate in and appreciate your tradition; it ratifies the sense of social solidarity that makes you human. At the same time it prompts you to appropriate that tradition in your own way in response to the gifts of the Holy Spirit, and to contribute your special form of faith-sense to the tradition for the sake of others. This last point leads to the preeminent reason why making faith-sense is worth the effort.

SPIRITUAL WHOLENESS

We make faith-sense because we are spiritual beings made in the image of God. We belong to one another and find fulfillment in being together as a reflection of God's trinitarian life. The inner life of the Trinity is a distinctive mystery of Christian belief. It has been revealed to us through the activity of the three divine Persons in human history. God the Father proposes ideals for creative living, beginning with the idea of creation itself. God the Son (or Word) responds to these ideals, incarnating the perfection of God the Father's desires in human experience. God the Holy Spirit unifies and sustains this interaction, not only between the divine persons but also among all the creatures made in God's image.

In short, the Spirit harmonizes the ideals we envision from the Father with the practical outcomes we achieve in and through the Son. This does not mean that everything fits together perfectly. Whatever harmony or value there is, the Spirit confirms and makes part of the ongoing life of creation and of God. This is not only a creative work; it is also extremely personal.

The Spirit relates to you in your individuality and uniqueness. The opportunities and gifts which distinguish you are what the Spirit seeks out and works with. This is precisely where faith-sense occurs. It is a constantly creative task, weaving ideals and actual events into the whole that is your life of faith. The Spirit, of course, does not do all the work. The Spirit prompts, guides, instructs, and urges, but you must make your own faith-sense. And when you do, it becomes part of God's experience as the Spirit mediates the actual realization of God's ideals in your life and feeds them into God's experience of the world.

For all these reasons, making faith-sense is always worth the effort. It is the way you shape your life as a whole into the image of God, as the image of God. It satisfies your rational nature, secures your emotional makeup, and strengthens your social solidarity. Most of all, it makes a lasting contribution to God and verifies the divine image in you and all of creation.